# The Ecolodge Sourcebook

## for Planners & Developers

Edited by

*Donald E. Hawkins*
*Director, International Institute of Tourism Studies*
*The George Washington University*

*Megan Epler Wood*
*Executive Director, The Ecotourism Society*

*Sam Bittman*
*President, BMG, Inc.*

THE ECOTOURISM SOCIETY

*The Ecotourism Society*
*North Bennington, Vermont*

Library of Congress Catalog Card Number 95-060624

ISBN 0-9636331-1-2

Production Director: Sam Bittman
Designer: Meg Scrafford, BMG, Inc.
Cover Design: Meg Scrafford
Cover Illustration: Michael Chun, Wimberly, Allison, Tong & Goo, Architects
Copy Editors: Sarah Novak, Sam Bittman

# Table of Contents

# Foreword

*By Stanley Selengut*

Nearly 20 years ago, I came to the island of St. John in the U.S. Virgin Islands from New York City with the intention of building a resort on private land within a U.S. national park. I knew little of sustainable design. Many of the residents of St. John and local government officials were fearful that I would destroy the beautiful property that I purchased. I was determined to prove to them and myself that this property could be preserved and still be developed.

I learned as I went along. We built boardwalks between tent cottages to eliminate all foot traffic impacts. Construction materials were carried along the walks. Tents were placed between the trees on hand-dug post holes. Utilities were hidden beneath the walkways rather than buried in trenches. We found that by recycling our gray waters and using them on the vegetation we could significantly improve the degraded landscape we inherited. Over the years, we found new ways to introduce more efficiency to our resort, reduce waste, and minimize impacts. It has been a wondrous project! I simply started a small resort, used my best instincts, and allowed the business to grow naturally. Worldwide recognition and success have followed to my constant surprise.

The learning path took me to the point I am today, with three sites developed on St. John. One hundred and fourteen tent cottages have been built using site-sensitive development at Maho Bay. Nine luxury units with a swimming pool were constructed using passive solar design and sensitive land use at Estate Concordia. And 12 luxury units have been built entirely with recycled building materials and powered with solar energy at the Harmony Resort.

From the very beginning, I believed that eco-tourism development was a pure art form, where the designer arranged all the indigenous cultural and natural assets into a guest experience. The ecolodge developer's palette consists of local plants and animals, music, dance, architecture, religion, history, costumes, crafts and all the features which make the resort location unique. This has proven to be a successful approach to ecolodge development.

From the outset I also knew that all Maho Bay guests should be able to express their own opinions about the resort. For 19 years, we have been sending all guests a questionnaire to their homes with a stamped return envelope to solicit guidance. These questionnaires soon provided me with good information on the "ecotourist" profile. Our guests were looking for no pesticides, peace and quiet, no hard liquor, no tipping, uncluttered beaches, quiet watersports, closeness to nature, health-oriented foods, pedestrian walkways, and above all an intimate interaction with pristine natural surroundings and the local community.

For years our artful approach to resort design and operations have found a remarkably loyal market at Maho Bay. We are clearly delivering what our customers want and as a result Maho's occupancy rate is one of the highest in the Caribbean – 70% year-round and 95% in the high season. But I am never totally satisfied. After years of finding ways to improve efficiency and reduce waste, I was fascinated by the challenge of making an ecolodge truly sustainable. I wanted to introduce new technologies which would enable our resort to be powered without the use of fossil fuels. I wanted to produce water and food without having to transport it over long distances. And I wanted to channel more of the waste from the resort back into the production of food for the humans, plants and animals on the property.

Harmony and its sister resort, Estate Concordia, reflect my approaches to these goals. Harmony is "off the grid." Electricity is independently generated by sun and wind power. The architecture maximizes these natural resources, using passive solar design, photovoltaics, and roof scoops that draw air through the well-furnished rooms. Guests are encouraged to monitor their energy use on computers in each unit. Construction methods minimized removal of trees and vegetation and the dwellings themselves are made from the most advanced recycled materials.

But Harmony units are expensive to build and all of the sustainable technologies are in many ways invisible to our clients. The showers are hot, the electricity turns on with the flip of a switch, and the appliances make life at Harmony resort seem a lot like home. Responses to our customer questionnaires immediately made it clear that our guests enjoy the comforts of private bathrooms with hot showers, refrigerators and overhead fans. However, they missed the close to nature experience provided by the Maho Bay tent cottages. It was quite amazing to me that my customers

preferred a $7,000 Maho tent cottage to an $80,000 Harmony luxury unit – but it seemed to be true!

I concluded that a tent with many of the same amenities as Harmony was the next step in my development path. These new hybrids were immediately dubbed "Ecotents." (See Resources, p. 132) They combine the economy and close-to-nature experience of Maho Bay Campground with the soft technologies of Harmony. They explore various forms of photovoltaic and wind energy, composting toilets, water collection, solar hot water, showers and energy efficient appliances. Space-age fabrics reflect the heat and protect the interiors. The low building cost of the ecotents allows for high profitability while offering an affordable, educational, nature- oriented vacation.

My goal is to demonstrate that an ecotourism facility can balance both ecological sensitivity and creature comforts. If my experience has taught me anything, it is that we are not separate from nature, but an intimate part of it. With that intimacy comes a profound responsibility. As more ecolodges are built, we need to be cautious that our enthusiasm for the product does not exceed the carrying capacity of our sites. I have always advocated taking a simpler, lower-cost approach to development, and have proven how profitable this can be. I intend to continue experimenting, and I look forward with great interest to seeing how "The Ecolodge Sourcebook for Planners and Developers" will help others to progress along the development path I began forging nearly 20 years ago.

# Preface

*By the Editors*

The First International Ecolodge Forum and Field Seminar was held at Maho Bay Camps on St. John in the U.S. Virgin Islands, October 23-29, 1994, to bring together the expertise necessary to ensure ecolodges are sustainably planned, designed, constructed and managed. What emerged and will continue to emerge are entirely new approaches to the accommodations industry which will distinguish ecolodges from other types of more traditional resorts. This Sourcebook is the first comprehensive source of expertise on ecolodge development that includes information on the international ecolodge marketplace as it exists, and on techniques for planning and design, finance and interpretation. Papers were selected from the Ecolodge Forum, carefully edited, organized and presented, to create this volume of resources.

There are no internationally accepted guidelines for ecolodges at present. The Ecotourism Society (TES) is undertaking the research and international review necessary to produce ecolodge guidelines in the upcoming year. However, there are a number of well understood characteristics. Ecolodges must be designed in harmony with the local natural and cultural environment, using the principles of sustainable design; they should minimize the use of non-renewable energy resources and avoid the use of non-renewable materials for construction; they should use recycled materials where possible; they should work in harmony with the local community offering jobs with a wide range of responsibilities and employment via contract with locally owned vendors; they should work to provide benefits to local conservation and research initiatives both public and private; and they should offer excellent interpretive programs to educate the visitor about the local environment and culture.

Very few facilities in the world presently meet all of the above standards. The purpose of the Ecolodge Sourcebook is to bring together the resources planners and developers need to achieve these goals. As the global market for ecolodge facilities continues to expand, it is vital that local implementors have the information necessary to meet global expectations and standards.

This book would not have been possible without the work of all those who contributed to the success of the First International Ecolodge Forum and Field

Seminar. The staff who work behind the scenes are often the unsung heroes of these events and they deserve recognition here. Kathleen Murphy, Ann Dailey, Cynthia Hawkins, Susan Buse, and Karen Jennings-Croombs all worked hard for TES to make the Forum possible. The Maho Bay staff also provided a tremendous amount of effort; in particular, Robert Carmody, Lisa Kaplowitz, Bobby Flanagan, Skip and Chriss Benvie, and Roland Kravats.

The sponsors of the Ecolodge Forum and Field Seminar also deserve a round of thanks: International Institute of Tourism Studies, George Washington University; Maho Bay Camps and Harmony Resort; U.S. Virgin Islands Energy Office; and American Airlines.

The co-sponsors also provided much needed technical support: American Society of Landscape Architects; Caneel Bay; Caribbean Latin American Action; International Trade Administration, U.S. Department of Commerce; Multilateral Investment Guarantee Agency, World Bank; Real Goods; USAIR; USAfrica Airways; and the U.S. Export Council for Renewable Energy. The U.S. National Park Service provided their excellent book, *Guiding Principles of Sustainable Design* – now out of print – to all of the participants.

Many ecolodge facilities are now being planned and developed. This Sourcebook should help inspire an expanding set of resource materials for this new generation of resort developments. The editors do not consider this book to be definitive. But the papers presented clearly demonstrate how much more information will be needed for this growing field in the future. New ideas and concept papers for future publications are always welcome at TES, as are existing publications that can be added to The Ecotourism Society Special Collection at The George Washington University in Washington, DC.

# Introduction:

# International Ecolodge Survey

*By David Russell, Chris Bottrill and Greg Meredith*

## Introduction

A product of the ecotourism industry is packaged lodge accommodation in remote, natural areas. This introduction presents the findings of a study of this lodge type. (*This study used a strict but useful definition of an ecolodge. It does not necessarily represent The Ecotourism Society's views. Eds.*) The study objectives included identification of:

- Successful and/or unique examples of nature-based lodges;

- ingredients of lodge success;

- methods of management and operation;

- issues of difficulty and concern faced by the industry;

- planning structures to administer lodge development;

- industry resource needs;

- customer demands; and

- market trends.

## *Methodology*

A qualitative assessment of lodge development and operation involved the following stages of research:

- Literature search on nature-based lodges;

- identification and inventory of lodges;

- networking to identify successful lodges through travel agencies, wholesalers, tour operators and individual travelers;

- telephone interviews with operators of 28 lodges in 12 countries throughout the world;

- collection of marketing material from lodges participating in the survey;

- synthesis of information.

The ecolodge operators interviewed represent diverse geographic area as shown below.

| Country | No. of Ecolodge Operators Interviewed |
|---------|:---:|
| Belize | 4 |
| Costa Rica | 3 |
| Peru | 7 |
| Brazil | 1 |

| | |
|---|---|
| Ecuador | 1 |
| Alaska | 1 |
| Australia | 4 |
| New Zealand | 2 |
| Africa | 5 |
| **Total** | **28** |

## Market Profile

### Terminology

The term "ecolodge" is an industry label used to identify a nature-dependent tourist lodge that meets the philosophy and principles of ecotourism. At a purist level an ecolodge will offer a tourist an educational and participatory experience, be developed and managed in an environmentally sensitive manner and protect its operating environment (Bottrill and Pearce, 1995). A more generic term is "nature-based lodge" which, although useful for those uncomfortable with the popularized "eco" label, does not distinguish a tourist lodge from those representative of the mainstream; for example, fishing and ski lodges and luxury retreats (Exhibit 1.1). Ecolodges are often marketed under names relating to location, such as the BinnaBurra Mountain Lodge. However, it is the philosophy of ecological sensitivity that must underlie, and ultimately define, each operation. It is this philosophy that the client is seeking both from the lodge operator and from government in their support of resource conservation.

In this report the term ecolodge is used, as the concept and aims of such lodge development was considered consistent with market expectations, trends, industry supply and product potential.

### Distribution and Supply

Key areas of ecolodge development include Belize; Costa Rica; Ecuador; Iquitos and Cuzco, Peru; Manaus, Brazil; Queensland, Australia; Kenya and Tanzania Game Parks; Malawi; Botswana; and South Africa.

Belize and Costa Rica are host to several high pro-

Exhibit 1.1: *Traditional Lodges vs the Ecolodge*

| TRADITIONAL | ECOLODGE |
|---|---|
| 1. Luxury | Comfortable basic needs |
| 2. Generic style | Unique character style |
| 3. Relaxation focus | Activity/educational focus |
| 4. Activities are facility-based, e.g., golf, tennis, swimming pools, gymnasiums | Activities are nature/recreation-based, e.g., hiking, snorkeling, diving, sea kayaking, horse trekking |
| 5. Enclave development | Integrated development with local environment |
| 6. Group/consortium ownership common | Individual ownership common |
| 7. Profit maximization based on high guest capacity, services and prices | Profit maximization based on strategic design, location, low capacity, services, price |
| 8. High investment | Moderate/low investment |
| 9. Key attractions are facility and surroundings | Key attractions are surroundings and facility |
| 10. Gourmet meals, service and presentation | Good/hearty meals and service, often a cultural influence |
| 11. Market within chain | Market (normally) independently |
| 12. Guides and nature interpreters nonexistent or minor feature of operation | Guides and nature interpreters focus of operation |

file ecolodges. The research indicates the product in both locations may have reached a point of saturation. Both the Belize and Costa Rican governments have been proactive in their approach to resource management by protecting 38% and 30% respectively of the land base. The industry, however, has not been regulated in either jurisdiction, and in an attempt to make a profit, operators are now needing to diversify their product to remain distinctive in the marketplace. Another problem for Costa Rica is that of increasing crime. This issue, raised by several operators in the Central American region, could have devastating consequences for their international market image.

The majority of ecolodges in Ecuador, Peru and Brazil are in the Amazon basin, and are subject to access, safety and country image issues rather than those of resource use conflict and protection. Peru in particular has suffered since 1990 when the U.S. State Department issued a warning not to travel there due to terrorism. This single action almost forced operators out of business. They are now pricing competitively to regain ground in the industry, but their experience again demonstrates the importance of a positive international image.

Very few ecolodges exist in North America, as the markets appear to favor independent camping and/or comfortable recreational lodges. In Australia, the highest ecolodge concentration is in the Cape York region of northern Queensland. While the tourist perception of Australia may be of dry deserts and surfing beaches, this region shares many characteristics with other ecotourism destinations including rainforests, bird life, coral reefs and a warm climate.

Established and extensive wildlife viewing lodges operate in Kenya and Tanzania, and there are a variety of new developments in Botswana, Malawi and the Natal and eastern Transvaal regions of South Africa. Controlling interests tend to lie with large domestic and international companies, which have strategic economic advantages in lobbying for resource needs. From this, intriguing and unique management options involving three-party vested interests have emerged.

A brief overview of the international supply of ecolodges produces a range of issues for discussion, each aimed at identifying the key for business success.

## The Ecolodge Product

Product refers to the experience a tourist receives from what the operator supplies. Several factors constitute the tourism product. In the case of an ecolodge, key factors relate to location, natural and cultural attractions, facilities, food, activities and general atmosphere. From a marketing perspective an operator will try to sum up these factors in a few sentences. For example:

"Our lodge sits high amongst the mountain tops where the air is crisp and fresh. Delightful timber, stone and shingle cabins nestle unobtrusively into the hillside. To make sure you forget about the world you left behind, there is no phone in your room, no clock, no TV. At (our lodge), you'll find a true holiday retreat – a place that caters not only to your every need, but to your spirit as well."

"Deep in virgin forest, our lodge is necessarily remote. But with dugout canoes, with horses and with brute manual labor we have brought to this paradise as much luxury as possible." ... "(We) offer the kind of hospitality and service you would expect from the best American bed and breakfast places. The food is fine, the ambiance about exotic as it gets and the locals are friendly. At (our lodge), anything is possible."

"(We have) a place to see and learn about wildlife, to witness the splendors of Denali and the Alaska range and to explore the marvels of this sub-arctic ecosystem. Though surrounded by a national park and located at the end of a remote road, (our) back-country lodge is also unexpectedly comfortable. Cozy cabins and a spacious lodge provide a relaxed setting for exploring and learning about the surrounding wild country."

Exhibit 1.2 summarizes the key product characteristics reported by operators surveyed. From this and other research, an overview of ecolodge product is identified as follows.

### Location and Resource Protection

Protection of an ecolodge's operational environment is critical to operation. Such protection rests ultimately in the hands of government, and will determine long-term investment security, visitor appreciation and destination image. Options for protection include national parks, nature reserves and the recognition of tourism needs in national land- and water-based planning. The operator survey demonstrates that virtually all operations are based in protected areas. Administrative policy and concession procedures usually deter development within national parks so many operators own small pockets of land on park fringes or within more flexibly administered nature reserves.

Within these natural environments, operations are relatively isolated. This has the dual effect of positioning a tourist in a unique and rich natural environment away from the impact of civilization, and providing a feeling of "being somewhere different." While isolation is a product of access distance and difficulty, it may also be a psychological impression made for the individual by the atmosphere of the lodge operation. Many operations promote the feeling of isolation by using traditional ground transportation means such as dugout canoe transfers to lodges. This creates a nature excursion in itself; it minimizes disturbance of wildlife and provides an immediate impression of authenticity, remoteness and unique appeal for the tourist. The importance of isolation was demonstrated by an Australian company that owns two lodges of very similar design, run under the same principles, and each with unique environments of mountain and lowland forest respectively. The first lodge, however, is only a one-and-a-half hour drive from a major urban center, and is suffering relatively low occupation. The second lodge, however, is eight hours from a more remote and smaller community, and is highly successful. The image of isolation is reported by operators as important for success. Notably, the term "wilderness" appears in the marketing literature of 24 of the 28 lodges surveyed.

### Natural Attractions

Several operators commented that the key to success was an environment of outstanding natural beauty. African savannah, the Amazon basin and Alaskan wilderness are prime examples. While quality attractions are a vital ingredient for the destination, the quality and character of the operation will be the true measure of success. On this basis, operations in Belize, New Zealand and the Caribbean have succeeded well in attractive, but not necessarily internationally renowned, locations.

From a diverse range of geographical locations, 24 operations identified wildlife viewing (including bird and marine life) as important features of the nature experience. The importance of wildlife for adding character to the operational environment is demonstrated regularly in activities and design features such as elevated accommodations and walkways.

Cultural attractions took second stage to nature, but also contributed to character. Many operators incorporated local cultural resources in personnel, activity interpretation programs, and in design and decor of their facilities.

### Facilities

The marketplace recognizes the ecolodge by distinct design features, intended primarily to blend in with the natural area. These features relate to both the site and building facilities.

Sustainable site design requires holistic, ecologically based strategies to create projects that do not alter but instead restore existing site systems such as plant and animal communities, soils and hydrology (USDI, 1993).

Facility design can act as a key determinant of market appeal and should represent its environment with tact and with ingenuity. An ideal design would be a construction of natural sustainable materials collected on site, generating its own energy from renewable sources such as solar or bio-gas and managing its own waste. Aesthetically, facilities should blend in with the natural surroundings and incorporate local cultural characteristics where appropriate.

The majority of operations featured lodge and cottage facilities. Within the lodge, a restaurant and bar were common with a large patio or veranda to act as a social gathering point for guests. In some marketing brochures, this patio was featured as a key attraction to demonstrate the friendly atmosphere of the lodge. While bars and alcohol were tastefully promoted in most operations, one successful lodge in Belize made the conscious decision not to feature a bar. For many, though, alcohol sales are an important part of business. As one operator in New Zealand commented, "We still make more money out of beer sales than we do out of guided walks!"

Cottages generally featured private facilities and

*Exhibit 1.2: Key Ecolodge Product Features*

| | Belize 1 | 2 | 3 | 4 | Costa Rica 1 | 2 | 3 | Peru 1 | 2 | 3 | 4 | 5 | 6 | 7 | Brazil | Ecuador | Alaska | Australia 1 | 2 | 3 | 4 | New Zealand 1 | 2 | Africa 1 | 2 | 3 | 4 | 5 | Total |
|---|---|---|---|---|---|---|---|---|---|---|---|---|---|---|---|---|---|---|---|---|---|---|---|---|---|---|---|---|---|
| **PRODUCT** | | | | | | | | | | | | | | | | | | | | | | | | | | | | | |
| **Location:** | | | | | | | | | | | | | | | | | | | | | | | | | | | | | |
| National Park | | | | | | • | • | | | | | | | | | | • | | • | • | | | • | | | | | | 7 |
| Nature Reserve | | • | • | • | | | • | • | • | • | • | • | • | • | • | • | | • | | | | | • | • | • | • | • | • | 20 |
| Forest/Jungle | | • | • | • | • | • | • | • | • | • | • | • | • | • | • | • | | • | • | • | • | • | • | | | | | | 21 |
| Savannah | | | | | | | | | | | | | | | | | | | | | | | | • | • | • | • | • | 5 |
| Coastal | • | | | | | | • | | | | | | | | | | | | | | | • | • | | | | | | 4 |
| Isolated | | • | • | | • | • | • | • | • | • | • | • | • | • | • | • | • | • | | | • | | • | • | • | • | • | • | 24 |
| Wilderness | • | • | | | • | • | • | • | • | • | • | • | • | • | • | • | • | • | | | • | | • | • | • | • | • | • | 25 |
| | | | | | | | | | | | | | | | | | | | | | | | | | | | | | |
| **Natural Attractions:** | | | | | | | | | | | | | | | | | | | | | | | | | | | | | |
| Rainforest/Jungle | • | • | • | • | | • | • | • | • | • | • | • | • | • | • | • | | • | • | • | | | • | | | | | | 19 |
| Mountains | • | • | • | • | | • | | | | | | | | | | | • | | | • | | | • | | | | | | 8 |
| Coastal/Lagoon | • | | | | | | • | | | | | | | | | | | • | | | | • | • | | | | | | 5 |
| Mangroves | • | | | | | | • | | | | | | | | | | | | | | | | | | | | | | 2 |
| River | | | • | | | | • | • | • | • | • | • | • | • | • | • | | | | | | | | | | | | | 11 |
| Caves/Geology | • | • | | • | | | | | | | | | | | | | | | | | | | • | | | | | | 4 |
| Wildlife | • | • | • | • | • | • | • | • | • | • | • | • | • | • | • | • | • | • | • | | • | | • | • | • | • | • | • | 26 |
| Marine Life | • | | | | | | • | | | | | | | | • | • | | • | | | | | • | | | | | | 6 |
| Bird Life | • | • | • | • | • | • | • | • | • | • | • | • | • | • | • | • | | • | • | | • | | • | • | • | • | • | • | 27 |
| Cultural | • | • | • | • | | | | • | • | • | • | • | • | • | • | • | | • | | • | | | | • | • | • | • | • | 20 |
| | | | | | | | | | | | | | | | | | | | | | | | | | | | | | |
| **Facilities:** | | | | | | | | | | | | | | | | | | | | | | | | | | | | | |
| Lodge/s alone | • | | | | | • | | | | | • | • | | | | | | | | | | | • | | | | | | 5 |
| Lodge and Cottages | | • | • | • | | | • | • | • | | | • | • | • | • | • | | • | • | • | • | | | • | • | • | • | • | 21 |
| Lodge 'n' Tent Camp | | | | | • | | | | | • | | | | | | | | | | | | | | | | | | | 2 |
| Restaurant/Cafe | • | • | | | | • | • | • | • | | • | | • | • | • | • | | • | • | • | • | • | • | • | • | • | • | • | 23 |
| Dining Hall | | | • | • | • | | | | • | | • | | • | | | • | | | | | | | | | | | | | 7 |
| Bar | • | • | • | | • | • | • | • | • | | • | | • | • | • | • | • | • | • | • | • | • | • | • | • | • | • | • | 25 |
| Electricity in Lodge | | • | • | • | | • | • | • | • | | • | | • | • | • | • | • | • | • | • | • | • | • | • | • | • | • | • | 24 |
| Electricity in Rooms | | • | • | • | | • | • | • | • | | • | | • | • | • | • | • | • | • | • | • | • | | | | | | | 19 |
| Private Washrooms etc. | • | • | • | • | | • | • | • | • | | • | | • | • | • | • | • | • | • | • | • | • | • | • | • | • | • | • | 25 |
| Room Telephones | | | | | | | | | | | | | | | | | | • | | | | • | | | | | | | 2 |
| TV | | • | | | | | | | | | | | | | | | | • | | | | • | • | | | | | | 4 |
| Air Conditioning | | | | | | | | | | | | | | | | | | • | | | | | | | | | | | 1 |
| Fans in Rooms | • | | | • | | • | • | • | • | | • | | • | • | • | • | | • | • | | • | | | • | • | • | | • | 20 |
| Boardwalks | | | | | | | | | • | • | • | | • | | | • | • | • | | | | | | | | | | | 7 |
| Conference Facility | | | | | | • | | | • | | • | | | | | | | • | | | | • | • | | | | | | 6 |
| Educational Facility | | • | • | • | | | | • | • | • | • | | • | | | • | | | | | | | | | | | | | 10 |
| Patio | • | • | • | • | • | • | • | • | • | | • | | • | • | • | | • | • | • | • | • | | | • | • | • | • | • | 26 |
| | | | | | | | | | | | | | | | | | | | | | | | | | | | | | |
| **Comforts:** | | | | | | | | | | | | | | | | | | | | | | | | | | | | | |
| Luxurious (3 star plus) | | | | | | • | | | • | | | | | | • | | | | • | | | | • | | | | | | 5 |
| Moderate | • | • | • | • | | | • | • | • | | • | • | • | • | • | • | • | • | | • | • | | | • | • | • | • | • | 21 |
| Basics (tent camps etc.) | | | | | • | | | | | • | | | | | | | | | | | | | | | | | | | 2 |
| | | | | | | | | | | | | | | | | | | | | | | | | | | | | | |
| **Atmosphere:** | | | | | | | | | | | | | | | | | | | | | | | | | | | | | |
| Friendly | | • | | • | | | | | | | | | | | | | | | | | | • | • | | | | | | 4 |
| Relaxed | • | • | • | • | • | • | • | • | • | • | • | • | • | • | • | • | • | • | • | • | • | • | • | • | • | • | • | 28 |
| Flexibility Focus | • | • | • | • | • | • | • | • | • | • | • | • | • | • | • | • | • | • | • | • | • | • | • | • | • | • | • | 28 |
| Service Oriented | | | | | • | • | | | • | • | • | | | | • | • | | • | • | • | | | | • | • | • | • | • | 17 |
| Personal | • | • | • | • | | • | • | • | | • | | | | | | | | • | • | | | • | • | • | • | • | • | • | 16 |
| Family Oriented | | • | | • | | | | | | | | | | | | | | | | | | | | | | | | | 2 |
| Educational Focus | • | • | • | • | • | • | • | | • | | • | | • | | | | | • | • | | • | • | • | • | • | • | • | • | 19 |
| Activity Oriented | • | • | • | • | • | • | • | • | • | • | • | • | • | • | • | • | • | • | • | • | • | • | • | • | • | • | • | 28 |
| Sense of Place | • | • | • | | | | | • | | • | | • | • | • | • | • | | | | | • | | • | | | | | | 13 |
| Realize Dream | | | | | | | | | | • | • | | • | | • | • | | • | | | | | • | • | • | • | • | • | 9 |

*Chart continues on page xv.*

preferably a design that encouraged air flow to avoid the need for electricity and cooling. Only rarely did accommodations feature 24-electricity and/or telephones and TV. In most cases, the absence of such amenities was considered an attraction in itself. On the far end of the scale, tent camp operations have been successful in bringing clients even closer to nature. These operations usually feature a central lodge and roofed platforms with only insect nets and mattresses for sleeping arrangements. There are several successful examples of this style of accommodation, notably in the U.S. Virgin Islands, and in the Peruvian Amazon where one multi-lodge operation's tent camp is its most popular facility.

Most facilities fall in the category of moderate (or rustic) comforts which, although high standard for a nature setting, is approximately the equivalent of a one to two star urban accommodation. Five accommodations were luxurious (three star and above), which again is a relative scale, but provided these operations with a marketplace niche in their region.

### Capacity

The ecolodges surveyed were generally small scale, of around 24-guest capacity (Exhibit 1.3). This assures that the sense of wilderness travel was not lost, and human impact on the environment was controlled. The figure of 24 was often identified to provide comfortable accommodation for one 15-person tour group plus guide, and eight extra beds for independent travelers. In contrast, several successful lodges, particularly those in the Amazon, maintained that a capacity of up to 100 would not damage the environment when managed appropriately. The key to deciding optimum capacity lies in environmental assessment of each site, determination of limits of acceptable change and consideration of the type of atmosphere a developer wishes to create in their lodge operation.

### Food

Many lodges feature a "meals-included package." With this, hearty homestyle meals of a local cultural character are common. As many lodges are activity-oriented, the quantity and quality of meals are important for satisfying customers and generating positive feedback. Only in one case did an operator promote French cuisine which, although distinctive, is not in character for the region.

### Atmosphere

A friendly, relaxed and flexible environment is promoted by virtually all ecolodges. Within this, an educational environment is also encouraged, but is not always the focus. In ten cases, educational activity lay in the provision of educational facilities for research purposes and individual client interest; for example, classrooms, laboratories, libraries or interpretation trails. All but three of the operators considered education to be an integral feature of the experience, but in a manner that complemented relaxation, activities and fun. As one Amazonian operator commented, "Clients don't want to be lectured here, they want to feel like they're Indiana Jones."

In most cases, facility design and activities encouraged close interaction with the natural environment. This gives clients a feeling of being somewhere special, and imparts a "sense of place." This atmosphere is a key ingredient in distinguishing ecolodges from more generic "nature-based" lodges. Resourceful operators sought to capitalize on this factor by "realizing dreams" of individuals. One operator felt his task was to create an environment that meets the fantasy of the individual. Another believed success lay in providing "poetry from the owners," thereby creating a special experience and encouraging return visitation.

In many cases, operators felt there was no blueprint for success; each operation had to create an atmosphere appropriate to the the specific setting and ownership.

### Activities

Client activities normally involve a sensory experience with the natural and cultural resources of the area. The experiences enhance the understanding and appreciation of the resources and lead to greater support for their preservation.

The majority of surveyed operations are in forest or jungle settings. Therefore, trail hiking, nature interpretation, wildlife tours and bird watching were not surprisingly the most popular client activities. Introductory nature walks and lodge transfers through nature reserves are typically included in the client

Exhibit 1.2: Key Ecolodge Product Features (continued from page xiii)

| | Belize 1 | Belize 2 | Belize 3 | Belize 4 | Costa Rica 1 | Costa Rica 2 | Costa Rica 3 | Peru 1 | Peru 2 | Peru 3 | Peru 4 | Peru 5 | Peru 6 | Peru 7 | Brazil | Ecuador | Alaska | Australia 1 | Australia 2 | Australia 3 | Australia 4 | New Zealand 1 | New Zealand 2 | Africa 1 | Africa 2 | Africa 3 | Africa 4 | Africa 5 | Total |
|---|---|---|---|---|---|---|---|---|---|---|---|---|---|---|---|---|---|---|---|---|---|---|---|---|---|---|---|---|---|
| **Food:** | | | | | | | | | | | | | | | | | | | | | | | | | | | | | |
| HIgh Quality | | | | | | • | | • | • | | | | | | | | | | • | | | | • | | | | | | 5 |
| Hearty/Family | • | • | • | • | • | | • | • | | • | • | • | • | • | • | • | • | • | | • | • | | • | • | • | • | • | • | 24 |
| Local Cultural Style | • | • | • | • | • | • | • | • | • | • | • | • | • | • | • | • | | | | | | | | • | • | • | • | • | 21 |
| Western | • | • | • | • | • | • | • | • | • | • | • | • | • | • | • | | • | • | • | • | • | • | • | • | • | • | • | • | 27 |
| Other Ethnic style | | | | | | | | | | | | | | | | | • | | | | | | | | | | | | 1 |
| **Activities:** | | | | | | | | | | | | | | | | | | | | | | | | | | | | | |
| Trail Hiking | • | • | • | • | • | • | • | • | • | • | • | • | • | • | • | • | • | • | • | • | • | • | • | | | | | | 23 |
| Nature Interpretation | • | • | • | • | • | • | • | • | • | • | • | • | • | • | • | • | • | • | • | • | • | • | • | • | • | • | • | • | 28 |
| Wildlife Tours | • | • | • | • | • | • | • | • | • | • | • | • | • | • | • | • | • | • | • | • | • | | • | • | • | • | • | • | 27 |
| Bird Watching | • | • | • | • | • | • | • | • | • | • | • | • | • | • | • | • | | • | • | • | • | | • | • | • | • | • | • | 26 |
| River Trips | • | • | • | • | | • | • | • | • | • | • | • | • | • | | | • | • | • | | | | • | | | | | | 17 |
| Horse Treks | | • | • | • | | | | | | | | | | | | | | • | • | | | • | | | | | | | 6 |
| Mountain Biking | | • | | | | | | | | | | | | | | | • | | | • | • | • | | | | | | | 5 |
| Sea Kayaking | | | | | | | | | | | | | | | | | | | | | | • | | | | | | | 1 |
| Sea/River Swimming | | | • | | | | | | | | | | | | | | | • | • | | | • | | | | | | | 4 |
| Scuba Diving/Snorkeling | | | | | | | | | | | | | | | | | | | • | | | • | | | | | | | 2 |
| Archaeological | | • | • | • | | | | | | | | | | | | | | | | | | • | | | | | | | 4 |
| Swimming Pool | | | | | | | | | | | | | | | • | | | | • | | | • | | | | | | | 3 |
| Fishing | | | | | | | • | | | | | | | | • | | | | • | | | • | | | | | | | 4 |
| Vehicle safaris/trips | • | | | | | | | | | | | | | | | | • | | • | | | • | | • | • | • | • | • | 9 |
| Golf | | | | | | | | | | | | | | | | | | | • | | | • | | | | | | | 2 |
| Tennis | | | | | | | | | | | | | | | | | | | | | | • | | | | | | | 1 |
| Entomology | | | • | • | | | | | | | | | | | | | | | | | | | | | | | | | 2 |
| Cultural | | • | • | • | | | | | | | | | | | | | | | | | | | | • | • | • | • | • | 8 |

Exhibit 1.3: Capacity and Pricing

| | Belize 1 | Belize 2 | Belize 3 | Belize 4 | Costa Rica 1 | Costa Rica 2 | Costa Rica 3 | Peru 1 | Peru 2 | Peru 3 | Peru 4 | Peru 5 | Peru 6 | Peru 7 | Brazil | Ecuador | Alaska | Australia 1 | Australia 2 | Australia 3 | Australia 4 | New Zealand 1 | New Zealand 2 | Africa 1 | Africa 2 | Africa 3 | Africa 4 | Africa 5 | Total |
|---|---|---|---|---|---|---|---|---|---|---|---|---|---|---|---|---|---|---|---|---|---|---|---|---|---|---|---|---|---|
| **ECOLODGE CAPACITY** **Capacity:** | | | | | | | | | | | | | | | | | | | | | | | | | | | | | |
| Units | 8 | 12 | | 14 | 20 | 27 | 28 | | 28 | | 72 | | 32 | 50 | | 20 | 14 | | 15 | 41 | 23 | 50 | 20 | | | | | | 24 |
| Persons | 24 | 24 | | 28 | 40 | 54 | 56 | 74 | 52 | 40 | 144 | | 57 | 100 | 300 | 48 | 56 | | 60 | 82 | 46 | 120 | 40 | | | 20-24 | | | 62 |
| **ECOLODGE PRICING AND PACKAGE ($US)** **Price:** | | | | | | | | | | | | | | | | | | | | | | | | | | | | | |
| Single occupancy/night [1] | 77 | | 210 | | 38 | 101 | 84 | 75 | 135 | | 125 | 145 | 165 | 70 | 150-300 | 325 | | | 110 | 110 | | | 85 | | | 200-250 | | | 145 |
| Double occupancy/night | 105 | 175 | | 170 | 61 | 137 | 112 | | 135 | 160 | 125 | | | | | | 470 | 80 | 220 | | | | | | | 160-500 | | | 162 |
| **Package:** | | | | | | | | | | | | | | | | | | | | | | | | | | | | | |
| Nights [2] | 1 | 1 | 3 | 2 | 1 | 1 | 1 | 2 | 1 | 4 | 2 | | 2 | 2 | | | 2 | 2 | 1 | 1 | 1 | | 1 | 2 | 2 | 2 | 2 | 2 | |
| Accommodation | • | • | • | • | • | • | • | • | • | • | • | • | • | • | • | • | • | • | • | • | • | • | • | • | • | • | • | • | |
| Transfer from nearest center | | | • | • | | | | • | • | • | • | • | • | • | | • | • | • | | | | | | | | | | | |
| Breakfast only | • | | | | • | • | • | | | | | | | | | | | | • | | | | | | | | | | |
| All meals | | • | • | • | | | | • | • | • | • | • | • | • | • | | • | | • | | | | • | • | • | • | • | • | |
| Guide | | | • | • | | | | • | • | • | • | • | • | • | • | • | • | | • | | | | • | • | • | • | • | • | |
| Guide local tour | | | • | • | | | | • | • | • | • | • | • | • | • | | • | | • | • | | • | • | • | • | • | • | • | |
| Other Activities (number) | | | 3 | 2 | | | | | | | | | | | | | | 3 | | 2 | 3 | 2 | | | | | | | |
| Entertainment | | | | | | | | | | | | | | | | | | | | | | • | • | | | | | | |

1 The averages calculated for price equal the lowest rate offered on a per night basis.
2 Package nights presented illustrate the number of nights and relative components offered in package deals. Per night occupancy rates shown above are based on these packages.

package, providing immediate interaction with nature. Other common activities are all recreation- and/or nature-based such as river trips, mountain biking and horse riding. Only in rare circumstances were facility-based activities available, such as tennis courts and swimming pools. In these cases, inventive design to incorporate a nature experience was occasionally achieved; for example, constructing an elevated swimming pool among the trees. When possible, cultural and archaeological activities were included. These were not common, though, and purely complementary to the nature and wilderness aspects of image and operation. Most often, cultural communication lay in the skill of trained, local interpretation guides.

Activities, while in most cases educational, are more importantly a vital ingredient of guest enjoyment. Ecotourists, like all market segments, seek enjoyment and memories from their travels. The nature experience they gain is a combination of both intellectual and physical challenges that together produce a dynamic experience for enthusiastic feedback and growth in the ecotourism sector.

## Price and Packaging

Prices listed in Exhibit 1.3 represent average daily prices (US$) for single and double night occupancies. These vary within operations depending on length of stay, contents of the package, quality of accommodations and economy of the host country. Most lodges charge around US$130-170 per single night occupancy for accommodation, meals and ground transfer from the nearest center.

In Peru, operators have currently dropped prices to recapture a market lost due to a poor destination image. In some cases, prices are as low as US$70 per single occupancy and include guide services, transfers and all meals. Operators felt it important to re-establish confidence in the destination, and were setting prices simply to cover costs. Their example demonstrates the importance of containing or eradicating crime and other negative components of international reputation.

Pricing, therefore, needs to be scaled to incorporate costs perhaps not incurred in mainstream lodge operations but which are essential to ecolodge image and success. These may include:

- Isolation costs in transportation and supplies;
- purchase of environmentally friendly supplies in keeping with business philosophy;
- target and niche marketing of environmental consumers;
- outbound international tour company commissions;
- education and training of local staff;
- off-season maintenance in isolated locations;
- membership fees of environmental and industry organizations;
- activity development and maintenance expenses.

## Trends

With ecolodge popularity, operators are having to specialize their product to remain distinct in the marketplace. Efforts to achieve this include increasing the educational product and developing guest activities offering closer interaction with the natural environment.

The educational component normally rests with nature interpretation, ecology libraries and research facilities. Some operators are trying to maximize educational potential and have developed classroom facilities and research stations to entice school and tertiary education groups. This has the effect of enhancing local resource knowledge and exposing their product to a new market.

Several inventive guest activities have appeared in ecolodge design which, although potentially costly, have provided a market edge for some operations. Examples include viewing towers and elevated accommodations and walkways. Viewing towers reaching above the treeline provide guests with panoramic views; a successful example exists within the Brazilian Amazon and features a 130-foot observation tower, allowing guests closer interaction with wildlife. This same principle can be applied to elevated accommodations and walkways. The same Brazilian example provides treehut accommodations some 100 feet above the ground, including a "Tarzan and Jane" honeymoon suite. Another example in Australia features chalets built on a hillside, which are entered from ground level at the back and lead to a patio at the chalet front some 15 feet within the foliage. Treehut design also exists at Kenya's famous treetop lodge in Abadare Park and at the Shimba Hills Lodge in Shimba Hills Park. In many Amazonian lodges, observation rooms are a built-in feature of design which, while not reaching above the treeline, are consistent with the principle of low aesthetic impact development. Elevated board-walks and walkways provide similar nature interaction while avoiding interference with wildlife ground routes. In most cases, these walkways exist within the facility site connecting lodges and cottages. However, an elaborate example lies in the Peruvian Amazon where a 480-meter canopied walkway reaching 118 feet in the air has been created, opening up a new region of rainforest research and exploration.

Ownership has traditionally been independent and small in scale. Recently, though, corporate owner-ship is becoming more common. Examples include the P&O line in Australia, the Hilton in Kenya and, to a smaller extent, multiple lodge tour companies based in South Africa. The effective marketing arms of the international corporations will bring an extended mar-ket into the ecolodge sector. However, sustainable management principles of community reinvestment and the like may be compromised if purchasing com-mitments are based off-shore. Corporate ecotourism approaches pose questions related to consistency with the spirit and intent of ecotourism and the impacts on international market image.

## Summary

The survey findings reveal that there are many com-mon attributes constituting an ecolodge operation. Typically, an ecolodge might involve:

- An isolated and protected natural setting featur-ing forested environment with a rich and abun-dant wildlife resource;

- a facility designed to blend in with the local environment, maximize local resources and give the impression of "being somewhere different";

- a lodge featuring a restaurant with hearty food, and an outside gathering point (such as a bar) to enjoy the evening's natural setting;

- comfortable accommodations with private bath-rooms and lantern evening lighting;

- a friendly, relaxed and flexible atmosphere;

- a facility and operation which fosters a close relationship with nature;

- a recreation-based, activity-oriented facility, aimed at providing a learning experience for individuals;

- a moderately priced all-inclusive vacation package.

### Acknowledgment

The Ecotourism Society and the ARA Consulting Group would like to acknowledge the generosity of the Government of the Republic of Trinidad and Tobago for allowing reproduction of this report. The Ecolodge Survey was conducted during preparation of the Tourism Master Plan and Investment Program for the Government of Trinidad and Tobago. It is a sup-porting technical paper for the government of Trinidad and Tobago's Tourism Master Plan. The purpose of the survey was to document the key conditions which characterize this sector of the tourism industry and provide background information to support industry investment in ecotourism in Trinidad and Tobago.

Responsibility for this report rests with the ARA Consulting Group Inc. ARA acknowledges the kind contribution of ecolodge operators who participated in the survey willingly and with enthusiasm.

### Literature cited

Bottrill, C.G. and Pearce, D.G. 1995. *Ecotourism: Towards a Key Elements Approach to Operationalising the Concept.* Journal of Sustainable Tourism, U.K. (in press).

United States Department of the Interior (USDI), National Park Service, 1993. *Guiding Principles of Sustainable Design.* Denver, CO.

# Chapter 1:

# Planning the Ecolodge

# Putting the Pieces Together...

**Methodology for Site Evaluation and Establishing Sustainable Development Criteria**

*By David L. Andersen*

## Nature and Culture as the "Keepers of Tourism"

The new vision and loyalty to our earth environment described by the U.N. secretary-general in 1990 has been manifested in the development of ecotourism facilities. While the number of lodges based on this theme is only a small part of the international tourism industry, their impact has been large; numerous conferences have highlighted current success stories and new strategies worldwide.

With this intense interest, it is important to pursue such development with a degree of sensitivity that has been rare in the tourism industry. Part of this sensitivity comes from a thorough examination of a proposed site and a realistic assessment of a proposed ecotourism project's expected impacts.

## Site Evaluation as a Precursor to Development

The success of sustainable tourism development often hinges on the initial process of site selection and the establishment of development criteria relevant to that site. While there is currently a great deal of interest and excitement about ecotourism and sustainable development strategies, there needs to be a thoughtful planning process to assure a successful project. Part of this process involves site evaluation. One needs to be prepared that, in some cases, careful evaluation may reveal that the site is not appropriate for tourism development.

The beauty of ecotourism is the inclusive nature of the product. It is about nature including the human species. It is about building with nature – not overpowering it. It is about building with the advice and involvement of local people. It is about holistic thinking. It is not about having more. It is about being more. Native Hawai'ians often say: "Pay attention to the wind . . . listen to its voice."

With this inclusive approach, it is important for a development/design team to examine the site in a manner that not only identifies traditional issues in resort development but also illuminates the "invisible issues" ignored by traditional planning efforts.

These include questions that are uniquely local, such as:

- What is the cultural impact of tourism?

- What are the trade-offs for economic growth?

- Is the use compatible with adjacent lands?

- What are the limits of acceptable change?

- Who monitors the impact of the project after its implementation?

- Is tourism really appropriate for the specific site?

- If tourism is appropriate, how does it fit into the broader spectrum of sustainability?

The questions above can be answered only by local people. Government ministers, while often well intentioned, may not always be tuned to local issues due to the insulating phenomena associated with political office. To learn about the issues relevant to the people in and around a proposed ecotourism site, it requires the time and effort to inquire on a level that often is inconvenient for traditional developers. It is these insights, however, that allow an ecotourism lodge operator to create a uniquely focused tourism development.

## Soliciting Local Input

There are a number of strategies for soliciting local input and support. For example, one might hold a town or village meeting and encourage local families to come and express their views on tourism development. If a community is unfamiliar with the ecotourism concept, it may be beneficial to take the time to explain the principles. It is important to put tourism in terms that local people can readily relate to such as:

- Why do you believe a tourist would come to visit your area?

- What activities would you expect a tourist to be interested in?

- What concerns do you have about tourism in your area?

- How do you expect tourists to behave?

- Are there places and times you would not like to have tourists?

- Do you view tourism as a benefit or a detriment to the community?

- Do you expect tourism to change the area substantially?

- If an ecotourism lodge is built in the area, how would you expect to benefit?

While attitude surveys may have some merit, there is no substitute for face-to-face interviews and community meetings.

## The Development of Relevant Development Criteria

The identification of local attitudes and concerns about tourism development, coupled with environmental sensitivities, can help shape relevant development criteria for a specific site under consideration for ecotourism development. Such criteria should be realistic and consistent with the local resources available. For example, while it might be ideal from an energy management standpoint to pursue high-tech solutions, there may be more appropriate low-tech solutions that do not adversely affect the operational characteristics of the project.

Time-tested architectural motifs of local architecture can often be a rich source for contemporary inspiration. Local builders and craftsmen can be advisors who share their wisdom about local building standards and practical tips from their construction experience in the locale.

Development criteria should identify:

- Problem statement;

- project goals;

- facts relevant to the site;

- needs of the local community;

- conceptual themes.

The establishment of project development criteria, distinct and separate from the design process, is a necessary prelude to responsive design of an ecolodge facility. The criteria are the key to defining the design program in distinctly local terms.

## An Outline for the Preparation of a Site Evaluation Study

The following outline is a suggested framework for assembling data when preparing a site evaluation report. It is important to recognize that each site has its own unique factors that may require modification of this framework. It is intended as a general guide only and should not be considered a substitute for seeking the advice of a planning professional.

The format of the report is often a key issue if the report is to be submitted to a government body or a lending institution. Therefore, it is prudent to ascertain if specific content and format is required before starting the process. To the extent that the report is to be presented in more than one language, it is important to verify that any translation from the original language successfully communicates the concepts and ideas as intended.

The use of maps, photographs and other graphics are effective communication tools. Such exhibits go a long way to communicating the site issues. If photographs of the site are used, it is helpful to key the photographs to a map or site plan.

If other reports and reference materials are frequently mentioned in the body of the report, and significantly add to the clarity of the report, consider including (if practical) such materials in the report's appendix.

### Sample Report Format:

**Executive Summary**

*Introduction*
- Background
- Statement of objectives
- Justification for the report
- Contents of report
- Methodology
- Assumptions and limitations of the report
- Acknowledgments

*Introduction to the Concept of Ecotourism*
- Definition of sustainable tourism
- Philosophical foundation for sustainable tourism development
- Design and development themes

*Site Assessment*
- On-site inventory
    - the land, its history and "sacred places"
    - site ecology/geology
    - climatic issues
    - sight lines/views
    - environmental assets
    - site-specific sensitivities
    - environmental damage
    - environmental and soils analysis
    - suitability for alternate energy systems
    - site appropriate strategies for waste systems/recycling
- Off-site assessments
    - people/cultural assets
    - local demographics
    - economic/employment issues
    - crime and other perceived barriers for visitors and local residents
    - relationship to parks and protected areas
    - relationship to trail systems
    - relationship to scientific field stations
    - relationship to transportation links
    - energy sources
    - communications systems
    - political stability
- Relationship to local community
    - relationship with governmental agencies
    - relationship to other surrounding uses
    - community issues and perceptions

**Market Analysis**
- Review of tourism development trends in the area
- Targeted traveler profiles and expectations
- Countries/regions of origin
- Characteristics and behavior patterns of an ecotourist
- Local area traveler profile survey
- Current market demand and future demand
- Current awareness and perceptions of the travel industry
- Complementary destinations and proximity to site
- Potential for "tie-ins" for extended stays
- Identification of "urban base camps" or larger resort facilities
- Summary of market potential
- Market absorption rate

## Summary of Opportunities and Constraints for Sustainable Tourism
- Major opportunities
- Major constraints/limitations

## Proposed Land-Use Concept and Architectural Components
- Land-use mission
- Land-use concepts
- Architectural style
- Construction materials and methods
- Phasing
- Description of possible components
  - the base lodge
  - satellite lodges
  - interpretive center
  - environmental learning center
  - local product outlet
  - ecotourism programs
  - sustainable agricultural activities
  - sustainable forestry activities
- Facility programs/activities to be accommodated
- Projected building areas and probable construction costs
  - base lodge
  - satellite lodges
  - local product outlet
  - environmental learning center (ELC)
  - ecotourism concessions
  - agricultural structures
  - forestry structures
  - fixtures, furnishings and equipment allowance
  - vehicles
  - infrastructure improvements
- Budget summary
- Analysis of operating revenues
- Involvement of local people in planning and operation
- Involvement of conservation groups
- Involvement of scientific groups
- Involvement of schools
- Integration with "urban base camps," interpretive facilities, parks and protected areas
- Siting and separation of facilities

## Identification of Issues and Alternatives
- Implementation/phasing options/permitting
- Financial issues
- Barriers to effective implementation
- Limits of acceptable change
- Characteristics of a quality ecotourism operator
- Measuring success: Long-term monitoring, enforcement and evaluation of the plan

## Action Steps (assuming a positive site evaluation)
- Client/community approval
- Establishing a development entity/financing approvals
- Team selection
- Permitting/approvals
- Preparation of construction documents
- Bidding and construction
- Long-term monitoring
- Marketing program
- Suggested timetable for action

## Appendix
- Listing of referenced material
- Site photographs
- Abbreviations

## Building on Local Values and International Understanding

Before all is said and done in the site evaluation process, it is important to pause and look for the spiritual qualities that can often escape the ordered dimensions of the site assessment process. If one truly wants to attend to the heart and spirit of the land, it is crucial to be sensitized to the energy that special places emit. Often these forces denote a sacred place that local people can readily identify. In certain locales, these places may be part of the cultural legacy that should be respected. In that light, cultural links to the land may be part of the unique signature of a region. It is attention to these invisible factors that may prove to be key to linking the visitor and host in a symbiotic manner.

Talking to local people and spending the time to know the site is also key. While it is not always possible for an outsider to gain intimate knowledge of a particular site, if local residents are involved it can often make up for some of the deficiencies of an outside consultant. On the other hand, an outside consultant can bring a fresh viewpoint to the process, which may mirror or replicate the expectations of outside visitors. A marriage of insider and outsider viewpoints should result in a team that represents both the visitor and the host. This requires cooperation and coordination. In simple terms, it means that the development team must be kindred spirits willing to put their individual egos aside for the benefit of a successful venture.

## The Limitations of Site Evaluations

In the final analysis, site evaluation for ecotourism development is an important process if it is looked at from a purely scientific viewpoint. It is "due diligence." It is not, however, a guarantee of success. The process, while often well conceived and well intentioned, is filled with flaws. One must see that, despite a battery of computer programs that play out multiple development scenarios for anxious lenders, the procedure of site evaluation is but an educated guess. At best it offers developers the opportunity to avoid obvious blunders.

Any development involves risk. Presenting "reliable statistics" is only a game played by academics with nothing to risk. There are too many variables beyond the control of the development team to certify success. There are things one can do to increase the odds of success. For example, emphasizing the training and commitment of on-site managers and staff is a key factor to success that often transcends the quality of facilities and the natural attractions of a site.

The tourism industry as a whole is a volatile marketplace. One negative incident for a traveler or sudden political instability can dry up the tourism industry in a region for extended periods of time. In this light it is important to look at ecotourism as part of a balanced economy in an area. It's not the only answer for development. And, in some cases, it's not the answer at all.

## What Should You Do Next ?

**1. Get your boots or sandals on** and spend time (lots of time) on the site. *Get to know the contours of the site in the sun's heat and the moon's shadow. .*

**2. Hire a professional** to evaluate the site in your terms, his/her terms, the lender's terms and in the terms of local people. *Listen to a message that is not convenient to hear.*

**3. Plan for failure,** but also plan for the "downside" of success (pressure for more development). *Draw the "line in the sand" before you face the immediacy of these issues.*

**4. Talk to local residents.** Involve them. *Their commitment is a strong indicator for the long-term success of a project.*

**5. Ask permission.** Many projects fail simply because the developers failed to involve the proper authorities at an earlier point in the development. *Make the effort to know the territory.*

**6. Define the project in distinctly local terms.** Give the project meaning and substance based on insights into the local environment and culture. *Find the unique signature of the site.*

**7. Measure success from more than one viewpoint.** Define and monitor success from a varied and long perspective. *Ask yourself: "How will the children benefit?"*

**8. Keep your feet firmly placed in reality.** Understand that sometimes projects can gain a life of their own. *Remember that sometimes the answer is "no."*

## Summary

With the initial enthusiasm for the ecotourism concept fading into the hard realities of the difficulties in obtaining financing, the challenges of marketing and successes (and failures) of built projects, the value of thorough site evaluations and strong business plans is becoming more evident. The value of local involvement in planning and in developing relevant design criteria for diverse sites is overlooked only at the jeopardy of the project. In evaluating a site for a potential ecotourism lodge, it is important to look at ecotourism as but one component in a balanced economic plan.

In some cases, it may not be an appropriate response to a site at all. When ecotourism development is appropriate, a positive site evaluation alone does not guarantee success. A responsible business plan requires an artful blend of commitment and understanding of the ecotourism mission, exceptional people resources, marketing savvy and financial staying power. With these assets mustered, the benefits of an ecotourism development can be modestly rewarding in financial terms, and richly rewarding in the conservation of this fragile planet.

# Local Communities and Ecolodges:

## Preparation and Planning, The Keys to Long-Term Success

*By Ray E. Ashton, Jr., and Patricia S. Ashton*

## Introduction

Long-term success for ecolodge development ultimately will be dependent on the level and quality of the initial planning process. Integral to this preparatory planning is good site selection, detailed site plan and design, thorough business and investment plans and a creative marketing plan. However, frequently the aspect of planning most essential to the long-term success of the ecolodge is neglected: An extensive investigation and plan of how the lodge and its business will affect both the human and natural environments (Pew Trust, 1993). With the explosion of nature-based and environmentally based tourism over the past 25 years, many operators have made attempts to establish ecolodges wherever interest in such tourism lies and wherever land is available for purchase. These attempts are particularly evident in countries where successful nature-based tourism is already underway, such as Belize, Costa Rica, Peru, Brazil, Argentina and others. These efforts include indigenous peoples who have been spurred to action by some non-governmental organization (NGO), native and expatriate land owners who see this as a way to make money off their land, and organized investors who are most frequently from another country.

Since 1978, Water and Air Research, Inc. has been involved with various ecolodges in many countries. Our involvement has ranged from evaluating and using lodges as an international operator of nature-based tours to our later work as consultants for would-be developers or for national governments trying to determine the impacts of these lodges on their conservation systems and human communities. Throughout the past 16 years, we have found that successful attempts at creating ecolodges are directly related to the level and thoroughness of preparatory planning, most specifically with regard to long-range environmental and natural resource conservation and symbiosis with human communities. The emphasis of this paper is the successful methods of planning that incorporate local people and communities in the development of any form of tourism prerequisite to the development of sustainable tourism. All too frequently, this part of the process of developing a tourism complex is ignored or not implemented properly. When viewed in the long term, the lack of this effort frequently can be seen to lead to a decline in the quality of the experience at the lodge and eventually to the demise of the business.

## Reasons For Planning

We have found that potential developers of ecolodges, whether they are indigenous peoples or multinational investors, frequently display an attitude at the onset of the development process that their efforts will be good for the local natural and human communities within the immediate area of the proposed development. This apparent gut reaction seems to stem from the idea that a lodge will produce jobs, increase infrastructure and indicate to the local populace that conservation is good. In other words, they believe it exemplifies all the basic concepts of ecotourism. This attitude is not unlike most business attitudes in developed countries: "Development is good because it will raise the standard of living for the poor people." One only has to visit the "eco-examples" of a few years ago and walk through the decaying cabanas and early stages of vegetative succession to see the results of this attitude and its resultant lack of planning.

There are many examples throughout the world where such planning was not carried out, though you may need a guide to point them out among the rubble or under the encroaching jungle. Few really good examples of lodges have been developed with a complete plan right from the beginning, and some examples exist where a good job of planning was done almost by accident as the facilities were being developed. Investigations, including Ashton (1993), Brandon (1993), Faust (1991), Drake (1991), and Wells et al. (1992), revealed some of the reasons why this all-important planning often does not take place. These reasons fall into two basic categories, cultural and economic.

### Cultural Reasons for Lack of Planning:

- *The "big brother" attitude*
  "We are the business people and we know what will work better than the ignorant locals."

- *The low class attitude*
  In many countries, the ruling class and outside investors look down on local rural peoples, and it has been a tradition to plan and develop without input from them.

- *The superior culture attitude*
  Even well-meaning planners may lack cultural understanding of the communities involved or may feel that they are doing these "poor people" a favor by offering exposure to a "better" culture.

- *The "save the poor people" attitude*
  Stemming from a lack of socioeconomic understanding, these people feel that rural communities are made up of poor people who have no jobs or method of income to raise their standard of living.

- *The "they don't own the land" attitude*
  Developers see ownership of the land being developed as the only important issue and ignore the larger issues of impacts and ownership of natural resources.

### Business Reasons for Lack of Planning:

- *The "lack of regulations" attitude*
  No regulations require either planning, evaluation of impacts or formal agreements, so developers have no reason to expend the effort.

- *The "bottom line" attitude*
  It costs time and money to undertake such efforts with no immediate profit evident.

- *The "status quo" attitude*
  Always stick to what has worked before (even if the parameters are not the same). We haven't done it before in other business activities so why change now?

- *The "can't lose control" attitude*
  If you ask people's opinions they will interfere with the business and you might lose control.

## Planning: Assumptions and Misconceptions

The one common factor evident in all our discussions of lack of planning, particularly involving community involvement, was the tremendous number of assumptions and misconceptions on which development decisions were being based. These assumptions and misconceptions about the local people and their wants or needs, the local culture and the business implications of local involvement can be disastrous to the ultimate success of an ecolodge project.

A prime example of how assumptions and misconceptions can occur and how good communication with local populations can avoid eventual problems occurred in Honduras.

### Example: A Case Study – Honduras

Initial planning for a Punta Sal National Park (PSNP) included taking a main road right through the 300-year-old Garifuna village of Turnabe. Everyone assumed that the village would be thrilled at the influx of "potential customers," the opportunity to enjoy the benefits of "advanced" culture and, of course, the increased opportunity for employment. When I became involved in this project we organized a series of "town meetings" to get input from local villages and rural residents. I found that they were not all thrilled by the idea of an estimated 85,000 visitors per year (Ashton, 1993).

**Misconception:**

*All local residents wanted the park and the road because of the potential for jobs and income.*

Some villages in the area wanted nothing to do with the project. Others were excited about the prospects of ecotourism and what it might mean to them, though it became clear that misconceptions were not just one-sided. One thing that became clear early on was that the main road needed to be routed elsewhere with just an access road to the Garifuna village, which was located in the buffer zone of the park. The Turnabe included an excellent example of native agriculture and the idea developed to build a demonstration village there.

The idea of the demonstration village was established when we were planning the appropriate infrastructure for the required carrying capacity of tourists expected to the area over the next twenty years. During our studies, which included Turnabe, it was determined that the expected number of tourists would be extremely disruptive to the small village, and the experience for most of the tourists who would be coming to the area ultimately would not be a positive one. Thus, the alternative of a demonstration village was suggested.

**Assumption:**

*The demonstration village would reduce the impact on the Garifuna village itself.*

The demonstration village would be situated between the village of Turnabe and the national park entrance and would be centered around a farm currently being worked by the community. The idea was accepted by all of the members of the community and everyone was excited about it. The community wanted to build, manage and run the facility that would be at the beginning of a 12-kilometer boardwalk that featured cultural and nature sites leading to the entrance of the national park.

Some of our misconceptions and some misconceptions on the part of the Garifuna community became evident as we continued planning. We were discussing the development of an existing ongoing dance and culture program produced by the community for various social activities and hotels throughout the country when we discovered a problem with the workforce. Local hoteliers indicated that, on occasion, the dance troupe would not show up or that they would appear with only a handful of people to conduct the program. This could pose a real problem when the community also became responsible for running the demonstration village for an expected 85,000 tourists.

We continued our discussions, and a number of meetings were planned with the community to carry out the planning process for the demonstration village and farm, as well as the development of the overall management plan for Punta Sal National Park. When discussing how the demonstration village would have to be constructed to handle the number of tourists, we went over the tasks that would have to be performed in the village, the number of people needed to run the village and the hours when the village would need to be open. The community had no problem with these issues.

**Misconception:**

*The Garifunas were able to comprehend the impact of 85,000 tourists per year and the complexities of running a demonstration village; they understood the need for consistent quality programming and were willing to work the hours needed.*

During a town meeting, when we were discussing who would want to work on the project, a major problem became obvious: Available personnel hours to staff the demonstration village. This was brought to light by the question of how many people would work each day of Holy Week. During this week, more than half of the yearly 85,000 Honduran tourists come to the beach and thus would be expected to visit the park. Turnabe people also relax during this period or host their relatives, who come to visit and go to the beach. Virtually no one wanted to work during this week.

**Assumption:**

*Local people would want to profit from the tourist trade and would be willing to work during the times needed and for the length of time required.*

The fact that no one would work during the busiest tourism season brought up another point, one that was overlooked by the socioeconomist, by the person doing the environmental impact statement and by sustainable tourism advisors from several countries who had been working in the community. Within this community, work related to income averaged two hours per day per adult. This included the businesspeople in the community who ran the store, the bar and the bank. Further, the people already involved in the vital businesses were the ones who were most excited about working in the demonstration village. These facts made it clear that the village of Turnabe could not provide more than 25 percent of the workforce required to manage and staff the demonstration village. Worse yet, those people who wanted to run the demonstration village were also the people who were providing the valuable community services like running the stores, teaching school and operating the bank.

**Misconception:**

*Local people believed that they could run the demonstration village in the same way they approached their own vil-*

*lage businesses and with the same time commitment of only a few hours per day.*

Ultimately, it was decided that the demonstration village would be managed by the park, and individuals would be hired and trained to manage and staff it. These individuals would come from Turnabe and other Garifuna villages. The income from the village would be managed by the Punta Sal National Park Trust and would be used to enhance needed infrastructure. People who worked in the village would receive a salary. The historic farm would be maintained by the Turnabe community as it had been, and the park would share with the community some of the entrance fee collected from tourists.

The moral of this story is that planners need to fully understand the socioeconomic fiber of the community that may be affected by tourism development and that may in turn affect the way in which tourism can develop. In this case, chances were good that the demonstration village would have failed very early, simply because the people of Turnabe were not interested in changing their daily lives to work during holidays or longer hours, even for substantially more individual or community income.

The key problem of developing a business plan with communities is that we tend to plan and negotiate under the assumption that our cultural and economic values and work ethics are valid in all cultures. As the first park ranger for PSNP put it, "If we wanted to make money, we would move to New York. Many of us have. We are here because we love our life, we love our families. We are not poor, we are rich. I want to work in the park because I love it there."

## Planning Prevents Potential Business Problems

The primary reason for establishing a plan with communities is to avoid problems down the road and to establish a strong product for the tourists using the facilities. Our investigations have shown a wide range of problems from direct armed confrontation, labor problems and the loss of wildlife and natural resources to the degradation of local communities. These problems are of concern to the tourism business because they may result in the area losing its appeal to tourists.

Secondary problems include lack of trained staff, problems with government officials and problems with supplies and services. All of these problems can lead to increased costs, reduced profitability and inability to be competitive in the marketplace.

## Planning Prevents Potential Community Problems

Problems faced by local communities and people have been the subject of a great number of researchers including Cerna (1985), Kiss (1990), Poole (1989) and Wells and Brandon (1993). The nature and gravity of these problems change with the culture, the habitat and the type and size of the tourism facility. The greater the distance from mainstream economic development a community or group of people is, the greater the impact the tourism program or facility may have and the more difficult it will be to develop meaningful plans and agreements with the community. The potential cultural changes and problems with agreements are extreme with an indigenous culture that is not involved in trading with or making income from the outside world. The more a community has been involved in selling and buying outside their area or culture, the easier it may be to establish an understanding.

Some of the problems that may be facing communities as a result of ecolodge development in their area follow:

- Infringement on property/territory (community or individual) by the tourism facility and the people who may work there;

- changes in hunting, fishing and other daily activities;

- infringement on personal and community privacy;

- over-use of resources;

- destruction of natural resources;

- cultural change without appropriate planning, support or opportunity for adjustment;

- economic change without appropriate planning, support or opportunity for adjustment;

- changes in individuals within the community;

- loss of traditional services;

- development of a dependency on the tourism facility leading to vulnerability as economic and cultural changes take place;

- governmental regulation and infringement on individual rights;

- population changes and related impacts, including increased crime, disease and shifts in ethnic distribution;

- environmental changes affecting the long-term health of individuals and the community, including problems with water, sewage, solid waste, air pollution, hazardous substance exposure and noise pollution.

By developing a plan that addresses the business- and community-related problems, the results to the community and the tourism facility can be extremely positive.

## Planning Methods

The first step in developing a successful plan for dealing with local communities and peoples is to identify the best method to use for that situation. Commonly, we find that owners and developers go into communities, perhaps meet with politicians, lay out their plans including what they will do for the community and go on with the development thinking they have worked appropriately with the community to produce a plan. They continue this effort by negotiating with individuals about land, services and other items without taking into account whether or not this fits into the culture of the local community as a whole. In fact, the developer has not really established a dialogue that has involved the time or patience needed to breach the cultural differences. More importantly, what the developer thinks is a clear description of a project and its impacts may be so far outside the cultural understanding and experience of the local people that it is meaningless. This leads to misunderstanding on both sides. Rarely is there a written agreement developed between community leaders or contracts with individuals to provide services.

## Whom Do You Talk To and How?

**National and Regional Governments.**
Many national governments are establishing laws and regulations pertaining to the development of tourism facilities. However, rules and regulations frequently are ignored in favor of attracting economic development. This may lead developers to think that once they have received approval from national officials, they have carte blanche to proceed with their plans and no one locally can stand in their way. Depending on the country, this may, up to a point, be true. If the local communities are politically active and they do not want the development, problems could arise as the facility is being built. Many developers assume that the process of negotiations and permission is over once they have cleared the federal hurdles. In fact, the power of local governments can be very strong and cannot be ignored. Many countries have or are in the process of implementing land reform. The land rights of communities and individuals are important areas that should be carefully investigated before land is purchased.

As part of the planning process, national, regional and local governments should be involved and kept informed once the land is targeted, and as the project develops.

**The People and the Community.**
During the site selection process, local communities and people living in the area should be investigated. Just as one looks at the natural attributes and how they might provide for programming, one should carefully research the people and their culture.

A number of visits should be planned to the area and, if feasible, an extended period of time should be spent with the local people. This time will reveal important information, such as where the leadership lies within the community. The elected official may or may not be the chief advisor when it comes to making decisions or negotiating for the community. Be up-front with the people about the plans and elicit their help in exploring the area. Frequently, it is possible to find a local person to act as a translator and guide. Often, this is a person who has been recommended by someone in government and who has been able to go away to school to learn another language. It is important to find out about the individual and to determine if he or she is acceptable to the community. Don't use a translator whom you can't trust or who is not trusted or liked by the community.

It is often better to hire someone to translate and assist you who is not of the community but who is familiar with working in rural or indigenous communities and with sustainable tourism. This person will approach things with a different attitude from that of the developer, and their experiences in the bush and working with people will allow them to relate better to the local community. However, be sure that this person will be acceptable to locals; do not antagonize local cultural biases.

## Education

Education is a two-way street. Be prepared to be educated. Have an open, inquisitive mind. Learn all you can about the daily life of the local people, including the way they make a living, how they deal with the outside world and how they relate to government.

It is also important to educate the people about what you plan to do and what it means to their way of life. Indicate to them that they have a choice in the matter (assuming that you don't want to develop where you are not wanted). The key here is to take time and patiently approach your subject. People may not have a base on which to understand large figures or what they mean. Re-read the example about Turnabe on pages 11-12 and the steps it took to get past the misconceptions and to realize how much work had to go into the demonstration village.

The education process takes time and a number of visits. People need time to discuss what you have said and to come up with other questions and concerns as time goes on.

## Discussions and Meetings

Always be inclusive in your discussions. This should be progressive, from community leaders to special groups – i.e., if the community is larger and has a conservation non-governmental organization (NGO), a union of some type or other potential stakeholders. If a number of communities are involved in the immediate area, these should be approached in the same manner. Ultimately, town meetings in each community should be held before the time comes to develop agreements. Depending on the culture, often it is best to have a group of individuals from each community involved in the process of developing agreements. This will help avoid misunderstandings and keep the information flow open so that the community hears more than just the personal feelings of one guide or one individual.

## Establishing Agreements

The ultimate goal is to establish an agreement that will guide the relationship between the communities and the tourism facility. It will be important to identify all points that are important to the success of the facility and the community. Be prepared to establish very simple agreements that both parties can clearly understand.

Have a list of points to be established in the agreement and provide these to the appropriate people in each community. Give people time to discuss them and then have a meeting to discuss each topic very carefully. It is extremely important to note that, in many cultures and rural communities, people have a tendency to "want to please" and thus to let you hear what you hope to hear rather than express their disagreement. This may lead to an agreement that is not clearly understood and not agreed to, and thus it will be breached frequently. Usually, time and familiarity will overcome this problem. Once the people know and accept you, they will be more likely to express their feelings honestly.

It is important to be sure that the agreement is easy to enforce. Making complicated proposals will often cause problems.

Once the agreement has been developed, everyone should sign it, and copies should be made available to national, regional and local officials. The agreement then becomes part of the business plan for the tourism facility.

### Agreements: Individuals vs Communities.

Agreements with communities should deal with community and facility concerns, such as land, visitation and use of resources. During the investigative process of learning about the community, it is important to find out about labor practices, costs and what is considered customary and acceptable. Of course, national regulations usually govern these items as well.

Issues involving individuals from that community may not be of particular concern during initial discussions, but may prove to be of significance later. If community members are ultimately going to be potential staff for the ecolodge facility, then eventually they will be concerned about furthering their education and advancement opportunities. The possibility of these individuals leaving the community after gaining experience, resources and exposure to outside cultures will be of concern to the community as a whole and to the ecolodge management that depends on them as potential employees. Information concerning such individual issues, if provided early in the discussions, may establish important ties between the tourism facility developer and the community. Agreements should address some individual rights and benefits where appropriate. This ultimately can protect both sides, since local assumptions about what an employer should provide can be quite outrageous in some cultures, leading to misunderstandings.

### Agreements: Establishing an Ecotourism Council.

Part of any agreement should be the establishment of a local ecotourism council. The council's makeup and what the council is authorized to accomplish is important. One mandate for the council should be to establish a method of problem solving for both the community and the ecolodge operators. In the long run, this is in the ecolodge's best interest and will facilitate the long-range sustainability of tourism development in the region.

Depending on the community or area involved, the council may be made up of the various stakeholders, including community representatives, lodge managers, conservation NGOs, park officials and others (Ashton & Ashton, 1993).

Ecotourism councils can serve to distribute economic rewards for the community. For example, if the lodge has made arrangements for people to visit the community, then the community, as well as the individuals who guide or provide some direct service, should benefit. If payment is made to the council or if the use of monies is directed by the council, that may serve to avoid major conflicts or possible misuse by some individuals.

The management and owners of the lodge should make it a point to meet with the ecotourism council and local officials. Frequently, lodge owners are not involved on a local level, despite the fact that they have become part of that community. An attitude of being too important to meet with anyone other than government officials can lead to alienation from the local social structure from which employees and future government officials come. Frequent communications can keep small problems from becoming large ones. Also, people can work toward the common good with national government officials and others to protect both the lodge and the community.

### Agreements: Periodic Renegotiations.

Any agreement must include a plan for periodic review and renegotiation of that agreement or parts of that agreement. As the lodge and its program develops and the community changes, the problems will change, new ones will appear and what was agreed to originally may not still work for either party. Set times should be established to renegotiate agreements.

### Agreements: Checklist of Issues.

Many issues must be considered in good planning and may become part of facility/community agreements. It is difficult to develop a generic list of issues that may be encountered because they will vary at each location. However, the following are issues that are most frequently of concern to both the ecolodge and the community leaders.

### Ecolodge Concerns:

- Property rights, squatters, rights-of-way, easements, quality access to lodge site, directional signage, advertising signage;

- employment and labor practices and constraints during construction, operation and programming – where will workers live and will they infringe on the natural areas nearby, turning them into muddy, transient work camps?

- protection of natural environment and program potential;

- safety for property and tourists, laws and legal protection;

- political climate and political relations;

- access to resources, including food, water and services such as utilities, sewage treatment, police and fire protection;

- land use and change of land use in the area – will a mine or factory suddenly be across from the ecolodge in five years?

- access to communications and transportation;

- emergency services and contingencies for national emergencies;

- agricultural, forestry or ranching practices that may be hazardous to the lodge, its environments or personnel, such as use of dangerous pesticides and uncontrolled burning or clear-cutting;

- protection of ecolodge wildlife migration routes and traditional feeding ranges with protection against poachers.

### Community Concerns:

- Property rights and continued community access to natural features like beaches, lakes or other unique resources;

- privacy and protection of individual rights – will tourists walk through the village and peer in windows uninvited?

- continued use of resources, such as hunting game, food, water, farmland, timber, medicinal herbs, mineral deposits and others – will fences now restrict movement between areas traditionally used by local people for passage, trysting or perhaps gathering fungi once a year for an important ceremony?

- impacts from lodge operation, noise, air and water pollution, sewage disposal, solid waste disposal and hazardous waste contamination during construction;

- community improvement through program involvement;

- employment possibilities and job training;

- impact of habitat protection on traditional resources;

- political relations and lobbying efforts – will

there be an influx of money to upset the current political balance?

- protection against negative social and cultural impacts, such as interference with traditional sacred or ceremonial grounds, alteration of traditional social power structure because of outside influences, pressures to change local customs such as religion, dress or courtship mores and negative influences on young people;
- overt violations of local taboos or religious restrictions by ecolodge staff or visitors;
- contribution to local businesses, community development and services such as libraries, medical services, schools and museums.

## Conclusion

A well-planned and well-executed community relations plan is as important to the long-term success of the development of an ecolodge as any other part of the business plan. However, it is frequently ignored or approached informally. Without the involvement of the local communities, ecolodge managers may find that the once resource-rich areas surrounding the lodge, which provided excellent program opportunities, may fall to agriculture, suffer from overhunting or become settled in a haphazard manner by their very own employees. Misunderstandings between communities and lodges may cause labor and security problems for property and people. However, if there is an effort to establish a well-thought-out agreement and if there are ongoing open communications, problems frequently can be avoided and a partnership can be created to work together for the protection of both human and natural environments which, in turn, helps to ensure long-term profitability of the ecolodge.

*Literature cited:*

Ashton, R.E. and P.S. Ashton. 1993. *An Introduction to Sustainable Tourism (Ecotourism) in Central America.* Paseo Pantera: Regional Wildlands Management In Central America. 106 pp. USAID, ROCAP.

Ashton, R.E. 1993. *Sustainable Tourism and Local Communities: The Need to Develop a Businesslike Approach to the Problem.* Proceedings of the 1993 World Congress on Adventure Travel and Ecotourism. Adventure Travel Society. Englewood, Co.

Brandon, Katrina. 1993. *Basic Steps Toward Encouraging Local Participation in Local Tourism Projects in Ecotourism: A Guide for Planners and Managers.* Kreg Lindberg and Donald E. Hawkins, eds. Ecotourism Society. N. Bennington, Vermont.

Cerna, M., ed. 1985. *Putting People First: Sociological Variables in Rural Development.* New York: Oxford University Press.

Drake, S. 1992. *Protected Areas and Human Survival: Enhancing the Role of Conservation in Sustaining Society.* Fourth World Protected Areas Congress. IUCN.

Faust, B. 1991. *Maya Culture and Maya Participation in International Ecotourism and Resource Conservation Project.* First International Ecotourism Symposium on Ecotourism and Resource Conservation, Vol. 1. Ecotourism and Resource Conservation Project. Berne, NY.

PEW Charitable Trust. 1993. *Conservation Lodge Feasibility Study.* PEW Charitable Trust. Philadelphia, Pennsylvania.

Kiss, A., ed. 1990. *Living with Wildlife: Wildlife Resource Management with Local Participation in Africa.* World Bank Technical Paper 130. Washington, DC.

Poole, P. 1989. *Developing a Partnership of Indigenous Peoples, Conservationists, and Land Use Planners in Latin America.* World Bank Working Paper 245. Washington, DC.

Wells, Michael, Katrina Brandon, and Lee Hannah. 1992. *People and Parks: Linking Protected Area Management with Local Communities.* World Bank, Washington, DC.

# Reading the Landscape - Knowing What is There

*By J. Thomas Atkins*

## Introduction

We are students of the landscape. We acquire a sense of the natural and cultural forces that shape the landscape by systematically reading landscape patterns. In ecotourism planning and design, ask what the landscape offers to the ecotourist. Look for the landscape limits beyond whose thresholds the natural and cultural systems begin to break down. Identify suitable places and appropriate levels of ecotourism development. The balance between ecotourist experience and resource protection is an issue that ecotourism must continually address and monitor.

### Reading the Landscape

In ecotourism planning and design, a logical approach to resource inventory and analysis, system-wide planning, site selection and facility design is critical to success. It is essential that ecotourism creates "win-win" results for the natural and cultural environments, local citizens, the ecotourist and the developers of the ecotourism facilities.

The following discussion outlines the steps to take in ecotourism system and facility planning and design.

### What is There.

The understanding of natural and cultural resources should be documented on resource maps. If there is a systematic collection of resource information, a regional resource information base for ecotourism planning and resource protection can be established. Governments developing ecotourism areas should develop such data bases or require such data from developers for the privilege of establishing ecotourism facilities within their country.

### Limits of Place.

An understanding of the area's resources defines the environmental limits of the place. Approaches to resource development must be formulated that respect the natural and cultural limits of an area and fit the intrinsic characteristics of the area. Monitoring the condition of an area's natural and cultural systems simultaneously with the introduction of ecotourism activities is a critical planning step. This monitoring system can use the environmental resource baseline established during the resource documentation phase and can focus on changes in environmental indicators, such as water quality, wildlife feeding and movement patterns, vegetation succession and local citizen use patterns. The quality of the ecotourist experience also warrants examination.

### Management Controls.

After resource identification and appropriate ecotourism facility development, a system must be put into place, to manage the ecotourism impacts on the natural and cultural resources of an area. This management system must be an integral part of initial system-wide planning, site selection and facility planning and design activities. This system can focus on the number of ecotourists and their length of stay within a resource area and limit access to sensitive natural and cultural resources. Rotating the use of sensitive areas will allow for recovery. Ecotourism areas can be animal, vegetation and medicinal plant preserves, as well as areas for local citizen subsistence.

### Learning Opportunities.

Ecotourists travel for recreation and search for authentic experiences that incorporate learning rather than contrived entertainment. These learning opportunities should begin at the entry point into an area or country, and be a system that ecotourists follow on their journey. The information system can include information provided by guides and tour leaders, guide books and maps and interpretive centers and trails, and can also provide both orientation and interpretive information.

### Resources to the Local Citizens.

Ecotourism creates a new value to the landscape. Areas have value for what they are, not for what can be extracted and exported from them. Many opportunities are available for local citizens to participate in the economic benefits of ecotourism. Such participation can include developing ecotourism facilities, providing ecotourism services and managing system-wide tourist experiences. Local participation should not be limited to the service industry.

### *Bioregionalism*

The ecotourism experience starts not at the door of the ecolodge, but at the point of entry into an area. This characteristic provides both an opportunity and

responsibility to develop a regional system for ecotourism planning, design and provision of services.

Ecotourists experience landscapes as they pass through them. Each landscape has its own character. Each provides different learning opportunities and experiences. The understanding of a landscape occurs at several levels. The broadest is the bioregion, where major physiographic providences define a place. The next level uses subdivisions within bioregional areas such as major river basins. At the finest level, there are natural and cultural divisions within the subdivision. These smaller areas include specific landscape features like estuaries, river systems and agricultural valleys. This bioregional approach focuses on the resources of an area and develops an ecotourism system that respects and protects those resources while providing the desired ecotourist experiences.

The following projects present the three levels of identifying landscapes for ecotourism opportunities. Each project defines the landscape for resource protection as well as visitor experience, and addresses ecotourist needs on a different scale. The common thread throughout the projects is the opportunity for both the visitor and local population to know and appreciate the landscape.

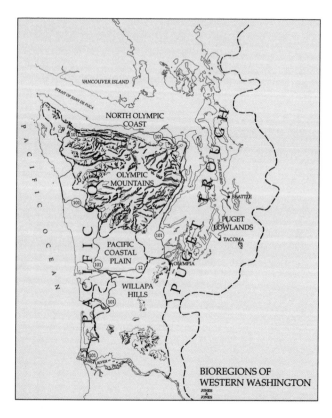

## Coastal Corridor – Oregon and Washington

The U.S. 101 Highway Coastal Corridor Study by Jones & Jones (subconsultants to CH2M Hill, Parsons Brinckerhoff, Quade & Douglas, Inc., and Parametrix) is an example of the bioregional level of planning.

The Pacific coastlines of Oregon and Washington are significant aesthetic resources, as well as important economic landscapes and complex natural systems. The natural and cultural landscape features of the coast define the intrinsic character of the area and are the main attractions for the majority of visitors.

The coastal landscapes were inventoried and analyzed as part of the planning process for the U.S. 101 Coastal Corridor Study. The coastlines of Oregon and Washington were divided into regions. Each of these regions was subdivided into biogeographic subregions, each having its own landform distinctions – climate, vegetation, water forms, wildlife patterns and cultural adaptations to the environment.

The state of Oregon has, over time, adopted a series of land-use recommendations and controls to manage land use within exceptional landscapes. The planning process defined landscapes within biogeographic subregions that are exceptional examples of each of the subregional landscapes. Exceptional landscapes possess the highest degree of expression of natural and cultural features found in the biogeographic subregion. For example, there are several dune areas along the coast, but Clatsop Spit provides the most intact example of that dune landscape type. For this reason, Clatsop Spit was recommended as an exceptional landscape to fall under Oregon's land-use controls.

Similarly, in Washington state, distinctive landscapes are now being defined. The analysis is focusing on the bioregional and subdivision landscape scales and is identifying exceptional aesthetic landscapes and existing and potential interpretive opportunities.

The project proposes interpretive facilities within each biographic subregion along the corridor. The interpretive system will include facilities that present information about the cultural history and distinctive landscape features within the area. Other system elements include interpretive signs, kiosks, trails and centers that will focus on the intrinsic qualities of the landscape, thus enriching the ecotourist's experience.

This network of interpretive themes and facilities will provide visitors numerous opportunities to understand the coastal landscape as they proceed on their journey.

## Green Island, Taiwan

The Green Island Natural Resources Tourism Master Plan developed by Jones & Jones and ECG International is an example of the second level in the landscape hierarchy. Green Island is a subdivision of the bioregional landscape of the southeastern coast of Taiwan. The area is within the East Coast National Scenic Area, administered by the Tourism Bureau of Taiwan.

Green Island was formally added to the East Coast National Scenic Shoreline in February, 1990. The 80-square-kilometer volcanic island is 50 kilometers from the Taiwan coast. Erosion has dissected the island's topography into a series of watersheds that meet the sea in protected coves varying in width from several kilometers to 100 meters. The island's three existing villages are located within such coves. A colorful coral skirt surrounds the island, providing world-class diving and snorkeling. In several cases, protected fishing harbors were cut into the coral skirt. The island's agricultural fields occur on the level plateau that forms the waistband of the island. Upslope from this rich soil are densely wooded volcanic hillsides. The lush native vegetation that once covered the mountainsides was replaced by exotic plant material, the result of many years of forest burning to provide a beacon for ships.

The Tourism Bureau's goal for Green Island is to develop the island for ecotourism so that visitors can experience the terrestrial and marine environments of the island without harming its natural and cultural resources. The master plan for future development inventoried and analyzed the island's natural and cultural systems and defined opportunity and constraint areas for ecotourism development. In addition, the plan identified areas for local village use, joint visitor and local use, natural system protection and environmental restoration.

The Tourism Bureau assisted in formulating the ecotourism development program. In general, the program calls for facilities for approximately 1,000 visitors per day. The proposed facilities provide many types of lodging, including tent campgrounds, mountainside cabins, marina and seashore lodges, golf course lodges and facilities within the existing villages. Bike trails and a bus shuttle system will meet the visitors' transportation needs. To assist in access controls to sensitive areas, the plan proposes to exclude rental vehicles from the island.

A majority of the tourist opportunities focus on the natural resources of the island. Interpretive centers with trails and self-guided hikes and bike rides will be an important part of the visitor's experience. A planned interpretive center-aquarium with underwater trails in a protected cove will introduce the wonderful marine environment to the visitors. Other program elements include diving services and floats with permanent anchorages to protect the coral, a water activity area with sailboat rentals and a marina. All program elements are located in suitable development areas.

## Mercer Slough Nature Park and Interpretive Center

The Mercer Slough Nature Park is an example of the finest bioregional level. The Park and Interpretive Center, designed by Jones & Jones, will be located on an upland portion of the 320-acre wetland nature park next to downtown Bellevue, Washington. This urban wetland attracts national attention because of its wild natural setting within an hour's drive of more than two million residents and visitors.

The Center will be the focus of natural resource-based tourism in the Northwest as well as a gateway to a network of interpretive trails planned along the Mountains to Sound Greenway, an open space and working landscape system that parallels U.S. Interstate 90 for 100 miles from Puget Sound to the Cascade Mountains.

The Mercer Slough Nature Park master plan defines the Slough's rich environments and sites the Interpretive Center on the edge of a small pond. Hiking, canoe trails and boardwalks radiate from the site, providing access to the Slough's environments. Natural and cultural information will be presented in the interpretive center and at stations along the trails. Viewing blinds will provide wildlife viewing opportunities. Wildlife ponds have been constructed throughout the Slough to diversify the habitats. Several of the ponds are solely for wildlife use and inaccessible to visitors.

In addition to interpretive exhibits, the Interpretive Center will provide an area for trip planning where individuals and educators can plan outings to other natural areas within the region. Classroom and laboratory space will be available for class field trips, where students can view the natural system exhibits before venturing out into the Slough.

## Conclusion

Individual landscapes and places are part of a larger system, where the sum is greater than its parts. Ecotourism must fit within this larger system. We search to define landscape limits and find suitable places for responsible ecotourist facilities and experiences. Ecotourism must create win-win situations that balance ecotourist experience, local citizen needs and resource protection.

# Chapter 2:

# Sustainable Design and the use of Renewable Energy

# Some Guidelines for the Architecture of Ecotourist Facilities

*By James Hadley and Patricia Crow*

The value of an ecotourist experience derives directly from the unique qualities of the chosen destination. The point in choosing to visit an ecotourist facility in the first place is to have the greatest possible participation in the climate, ecology and culture of the area being visited. Particular sights, sounds, smells; contact with unique plants and animals; interchange with humans of differing cultures in a spirit of mutual respect; these are the goals of the ecotourist's visit. They are worthy objectives in that they promote the conservation of existing places – landscapes, ecosystems, human settlements – and lead to an enhanced understanding and respect for these places.

The role of the architect in ecotourism can be easily understood and derived from the ecotourist's goals. The design of facilities for ecotourism will always seek to preserve essential qualities of place in sites chosen for development, and the architect may be asked to participate in the determination of these qualities and the appropriateness of development within the sites. The relative success of the architectural design will be understood as a quality of the final ensemble of structures, land, natural resources and surrounding cultural context; that is, to the extent that the architecture is a natural addition to the place in spirit and form, the architecture will have succeeded.

The discussion that follows is intended as an outline for those actively involved with ecotourist development and suggests a hands-on approach.

## Key Guidelines

### Site Selection and Design

**Quantification and Qualification.**
The architect may be asked to participate with other professionals – landscape architects, biologists, ecologists, anthropologists – in site selection for an eco-facility. Here, the architect must project impacts of necessary construction to determine potential change to the natural and visual resources of the site. Access and construction impacts must be included. A survey of indigenous building methods and materials can be helpful at this stage in devising ways of obtaining, delivering and assembling construction materials to limit unnecessary modification to the site. Judgments of appropriate levels

of development and potential disposition of elements within the site to preserve significant features must be made at the selection stage to assure that the site is not degraded by development.

**Deferential Design.**
Site designs for ecotourist facilities are consistent in their deference to existing site conditions. The site configuration always determines forms, layouts and routes of circulation. When there is a conflict between a site or building element and the site itself, the site always wins and the man-made element is distorted or changed to meet the demands made on it by the site. Generally, the planning energy is spent avoiding such conflicts, and in utilizing natural features as buffers, overlooks and focal points within the site. Major interventions to existing sites are only appropriate when a restoration of a site is being contemplated.

The ecotourist facility is also deferential to the existing cultural matrix. It is presumptuous to assume that local residents will welcome a flow of strangers who may unknowingly disturb routines or locations that are resources for food or culture and that have long had significance for local daily life. Planning the resort will include consideration of adjacent areas that may be disrupted by poorly located buildings or pathways.

**Reinforcing Existing Character.**
Successful site designs for ecotourist facilities will derive their strength from the specifics of the site (as do all successful site designs). In ecotourist sites, however, the site is the compelling reason for the existence of the facility and must be recognized as such by the designer. Determining the appropriate relationship of developed areas (walks, buildings, gathering points, services, access routes) to site features will be a major effort in the site design, and will include considerations of intimacy with, deference to, appreciation for and involvement with the natural features.

The relationships of the exterior spaces of the ecotourist facility will resemble as closely as possible those relationships that existed before development. In this way, the disposition of site components will more easily enhance perception of the landscape instead of creating a new set of relationships based primarily on preconceived ideas of functional needs.

**Utilizing Natural Resources of the Site.**
The existing microclimate of the site will contain a variety of attributes that can be capitalized on by the site designer. Patterns of breezes, sun and shade; cooler, wetter and dryer areas may all be found on the site and can be used in siting buildings and outdoor areas for human use to maximize comfort without artificial heating or cooling.

Many ecotourist sites will not have infrastructure for water and electrical distribution. It is of paramount importance that natural means for heating, cooling and water collection be used to eliminate or minimize the need for internal systems that rely on fossil fuel generators. Hence, orientation to sun and breeze, and relationship to natural sources of water (streams, rain) are significant considerations in siting of structures.

## Building Design

**Design with Climate.**
Clues to appropriate building technology in any climatic region will almost always be found in the traditional architecture of the region. The architect can look for responses to climate in relative thermal mass of traditional structures and in strategies for passive ventilation, heating and cooling. These were noted above in site design, but traditional building form, fenestration and organization will indicate direct architectural responses to climate. The design of buildings based on traditional models does not require imitation of these models so much as it involves extrapolation of basic principles from traditional examples.

As an example, the tent structures at Maho Bay Camps in the U.S. Virgin Islands are derived from the light framing of the typical Caribbean cottage, but carry the principle to a further development by using fabric – a lighter material than wood siding – to lessen thermal mass in a climate where storage of heat in structures is undesirable and the encouragement of air passage is important.

Relationship to grade is an additional variable in response to climate: Structures will be above and separate from grade in warm wet climates to avoid the dampness and heat from the earth, and connected or dug into grade in climates where the earth's thermal mass is of positive benefit.

## Design of the Construction Process.

The ecotourist experience presupposes a strong relationship between visitor and a site that is chosen for natural attributes. The architectural subtext to this relationship is that construction must disturb the site as little as possible. Construction materials and equipment must follow the ultimate circulation pattern designed for the site. Materials storage must be on future building sites or paved areas, and must be delivered in quantities that can be managed as described above. Any heavy vehicles used for excavation must have their movements directed by the designer to follow pathways, just as is done for materials and equipment.

Construction workers who build ecotourist facilities become part of the design process. Generally, a survey with accurate tree and natural feature locations is not going to be produced for a site in a remote part of the world. This places much of the final responsibility for locating structures on the members (or leaders) of construction crews. Parameters for siting of buildings must be articulated by the designer for use by construction workers. Perspective drawings or sketches can be particularly useful in showing designers' intent in relation of building to site.

When ecotourist facilities include photovoltaic power as all or part of the final energy package for the buildings, the photovoltaic system can be delivered first, before other construction materials, to power construction tools. This eliminates the need for temporary power lines or diesel power generation with its incumbent noise pollution.

## Simple and Appropriate Building Technologies.

The need to design basic buildings for remote locations is primarily derived from the respect for place that is central to ecotourism. The following elements are important in considering building technologies:

- How disruptive will construction be to the site? (as described above in the paragraphs covering the construction process);

- to what extent will local labor be a key element in the production of the facility? (Locals should not be the common laborers of the project, but should be to the greatest extent possible the "mechanics" or the skilled labor);

- will the architecture compete with the site for attention?

- how much non-renewable energy will the project consume in its construction? (This question is central to all sustainable buildings.)

## Design Metaphor.

Traditional resorts, especially in tropical and semi-tropical climates, are successfully described using metaphors that almost certainly informed the designers of the resorts, whether consciously or unconsciously. Leaving aside the large urban hotel as a formal type that is all too often repeated inappropriately in the tropics, there are two main types of resort hotels:

- *The Plantation.* This resort is characterized by extensive manicured and managed grounds, a deferential staff only partly visible to the guests and a site layout that establishes a central focus with informally disposed and scattered guest accommodations. The best known of this type are probably the present and former Rock Resorts in the Caribbean.

- *The Village.* These types of guest facilities are often hut-like, and site planning produces a superficial resemblance to an undifferentiated native village. This resort offers a fictitious sense of "noble savage" lifestyle, encouraging a relaxation of civilized tensions (and of responsible behavior). Typical of this type are the Club Med resorts around the world.

A more successful metaphor for understanding and designing ecotourist facilities is not a building type at all, but is the model of the organism:

- *The Organism.* Facilities are designed to respond as directly to climate and ecology as the plants and animals native to the site. Also, the resort should be non-hierarchical, with all parts equally important – building systems and services are as important as the visual design.

- *The Growing and Adapting Organism.* The resort begins at a fairly modest scale while adapting to the environment and the site. As the resort grows, original plans for design, construction and operation may be modified.

**Design for Ecotourist Management Objectives.**

### Trash Management

While the ecotourist facility may incorporate locally grown foods into its menu, management will likely import some foods, beverages and conveniences to accommodate the ecotourist and the staff. In a remote site, removal or creative reuse of the attendant trash will be done with ecotourism goals in mind. If management defines its objectives for this issue during the planning stages of the project, the site design and architecture can respond appropriately.

There is a range of possibilities for managing trash:

- The camper's guideline of "pack it in, pack it out." This approach requires storage, truck access and arrangements with a removal service. If this method is used, the ecotourism facility must insist that the service provided meet its objectives concerning the final destination of the trash.

- Creative reuse of the material. In addition to mainstream recycling, possibility of a local reuse or recycling initiative can be investigated.

- Limitation of use of packaged materials. This approach will still require consideration during the initial stages of design.

### Staff Accommodations

With facilities in remote locations, ecotourist resorts will often need to integrate staff housing into the overall site. It is important to understand that staff members in these situations will, of necessity, become part of the life of the resort in a way that is directly related to the remoteness of the location. Staff members of ecotourist resorts are often indistinguishable from the guests. If they are not members of the local population of the area, then they are likely to be people attracted to wilderness locations just as the tourist is. Hence, staff housing will resemble the guest facility.

Staff members, however, will need to be housed in an area that provides for individual privacy and escape from the demands of their jobs, but allows easy and immediate access to the guest area in emergency situations. They will need amenities that reflect a year-round rather than a one-week or one-month stay.

### Conclusions

Successful ecotourist resorts differ essentially from traditional resorts. Deference to and accommodation with natural systems have not been hallmarks of the resort of the past, but are at the core of the design issues of ecotourism. New developments in technology, especially solar power generation and self-contained systems for waste treatment, are powerful tools for the designer of these resorts, but the primary challenge to the architect of an eco-resort is to recognize the unique nature of the problem and to respond with designs that are discoveries, not reiterations. Native building forms offer a springboard to a new architecture that integrates the latest technology with local materials and methods of construction into what can surely become a new synthesis of architectural expression.

# Building Design

*By The United States Department of the Interior*
*National Park Service*
*Denver Service Center*

## Sense of Place

The concept known as bioregionalism is based on the idea that all life is established and maintained on a functional community basis and that all of these distinctive communities (bioregions) have mutually supporting life systems that are generally self-sustaining. Human civilization is an integral part of the natural world and is dependent on the preservation of nature for its own perpetuation. Over the ages, the complex interaction of natural evolution and human adaptation has given every place on earth a unique set of qualities that sets it apart from all other places.

Preserving the special characteristics of a place requires in-depth understanding of the natural systems in place and immersion into the time-tested cultural responses to that environment's assets and liabilities. In meeting the needs of the human community, development must be designed and built with an awareness of the relationships of natural, cultural, social and economic resources both locally and globally. Development must be limited to improving human life within the carrying capacity of resources and ecosystems. Development must not be an economic activity fueling the belief in endless growth. Thus the goal of sustainable development and sustainable building design is to create optimum relationships between people and their environments. More specifically, sustainable development should have the absolute minimal impact on local, regional and global environments. Planners, designers, developers and operators have an opportunity and a responsibility to protect the sanctity of a place, its people and its spirit.

It is the uniqueness of certain environments that creates the curiosity for tourism and the desire to experience their special relaxative, recuperative or recreative qualities. In providing facilities and activities for visitors, special care must be taken not to destroy the very resources or qualities they come to experience. This requires built environments that can sensitize and educate its users. Those responsible for park and ecotourism developments must recognize that by providing knowledge of the environment, they create the knowledge that is necessary to protect it.

## Sustainable Building Design Philosophy

Sustainable design balances human needs (rather than human wants) with the carrying capacity of the natural and cultural environments. It minimizes environmental impacts and importation of goods and energy, as well as generation of waste. The ideal situation would be that, if development was necessary, it would be constructed from natural sustainable materials collected on-site, generate its own energy from renewable sources such as solar or wind, and manage its own waste.

Sustainable design is an ecosystemic approach that demands an understanding of the consequences of certain actions.

## Sustainable Tourism Development

As ecotourists seek close involvement with authentic natural and cultural experiences, Aesculapian-based building design could establish a "rite of passage" to place human activities in harmony with local, regional and global resources. The resulting sustainable development would serve as a classroom to demonstrate environmental conservation understanding and respect for indigenous cultures and resources.

Following are criteria or standards that a sustainable park and ecotourism development should strive to meet:

- Provide education for visitors on wildlife, native cultural resources, historic features or natural features;

- involve indigenous populations in operations and interpretation to foster local pride and visitor exposure to traditional values and techniques;

- accomplish environmental restoration;

- provide research and development for, and/or demonstration projects of, ways to minimize human impacts on the environment;

- provide spiritual or emotional recuperation;

- provide relaxation and recreation;

- educate visitors that knowledge of our local and global environment is valuable and will empower their ability to make informed decisions.

## Sustainable Building Design Objectives

The long-term objective of sustainable design is to minimize resource degradation and consumption on a global scale. Thus the primary goal of sustainable building design must be to "lead through example" to heighten environmental awareness. Sustainable building design must seek to:

- Use the building (or nonbuilding) as an educational tool to demonstrate the importance of the environment in sustaining human life;

- reconnect humans with their environment for the spiritual, emotional and therapeutic benefits that nature provides;

- promote new human values and lifestyles to achieve a more harmonious relationship with local, regional and global resources and environments;

- increase public awareness about appropriate technologies and the cradle-to-grave energy and waste implications of various building and consumer materials;

- nurture living cultures to perpetuate indigenous responsiveness to, and harmony with, local environmental factors;

- relay cultural and historical understandings of the site with local, regional and global relationships.

## Checklist for Sustainable Building Design

### General Factors

**The design must:**

- Be subordinate to the ecosystem and cultural context;

  - respect the natural and cultural resources of the site and minimize the impact of any development; reinforce/exemplify appropriate environmental responsiveness

  - educate visitors/users about the resource and appropriate built responses to that environment;

  - interpret how development works within natural

systems to protect resources, foster less consumptive lifestyles, and provide human comfort

- use the resource as the primary experience of the site and as the primary design determinant

- enhance appreciation of natural environment and encourage/establish rules of conduct;

- create a "rite of passage" by developing an entrance into special natural or cultural environments that emulates the respectful practice of removing shoes before entering a Japanese home – visitors leave cars and consumptive values behind;

- use the simplest technology appropriate to the functional need and incorporate passive energy-conserving strategies responsive to the local climate;

- use renewable indigenous building materials to the greatest extent possible;

- avoid use of energy-intensive, environmentally damaging, waste-producing and/or hazardous materials; choose materials and construction techniques using cradle-to-grave analysis;

- strive for "smaller is better," optimizing use and flexibility of spaces so overall building size and the resources necessary for construction and operation are minimized;

- strive for minimal environmental disruption, resource consumption and material waste during construction, and identify opportunities for reuse/recycling of construction debris;

- provide equal access to the full spectrum of people with physical and sensory impairments while minimizing impacts on natural and cultural resources.

**Also, the design should:**
- Consider phasing the development to allow for monitoring of resource impacts and adjustments in subsequent phases;

- allow for future expansion and/or adaptive uses with a minimum of demolition and waste, with materials and components that can be easily reused or recycled;

- make it easy for the occupants/operators to recycle waste.

*Natural Factors*

By definition, sustainable design seeks harmony with its environment. To balance human needs with environmental opportunities and liabilities requires detailed analysis of the specific site. Although the following information is very general it serves as a checklist of considerations once specific site data are obtained.

**Climate:**
- Apply natural conditioning techniques to achieve appropriate comfort levels for human activities; do not isolate human needs from the environment;

- avoid overdependence on mechanical systems to alter the climate – such dependency signifies inappropriate design, disassociation from the environment and non-sustainable use of resources;

- analyze whether the climate is comfortable, too cold or too hot for the anticipated activities, and then which of the primary climatic components of temperature, sun, wind and moisture will increase comfort level (asset) or decrease it (liability).

*Temperature:*
- Temperature is a liability in climates where it is consistently too hot or too cold;

- areas that are very dry or at high elevation typically have large temperature swings from daytime heating to nighttime cooling, which can be flattened through heavy or massive construction to yield relatively constant indoor temperatures;

- when climate is predominantly too hot for comfort:

  - minimize solid enclosure and thermal mass

  - maximize roof ventilation

  - use elongated or segmented floor plans to minimize internal heat gain and maximize exposure for ventilation

  - separate rooms and functions with covered breezeways to maximize wall shading and induce ventilation

  - isolate heat-generating functions such as kitchens and laundries from living areas

  - provide shaded outdoor living areas such as porches and decks

- capitalize on cool nighttime temperatures, breezes or ground temperatures

• when climate is predominantly too cold for comfort:

- consolidate functions into most compact configuration

- insulate thoroughly to minimize heat loss

- minimize air infiltration with barrier sheeting, weather stripping, sealants and airlock entries

- minimize openings not oriented toward sun exposure

*Sun:*

• Sun can be a significant liability in hot climates, but is rarely a liability in cold climates;

• sun can be an asset in cool and cold climates to provide passive heating;

• design must reflect seasonal variations in solar intensity, incidence angle, cloud cover and storm influences;

• when solar gain causes conditions too hot for comfort:

- use overhangs to shade walls and openings; use site features and vegetation to provide shading to walls with eastern and western exposure

- use shading devices such as louvers or covered porches and trellises with natural vines to block sun without blocking out breezes and natural light

- orient broad building surfaces away from the hot late-day western sun (only northern and southern exposures are easily shaded)

- use light-colored wall and roofing material to reflect solar radiation (be sensitive to resulting glare and impact on natural/cultural setting)

- in tropical climates, use shutters and screens, avoiding glass and exposures to direct solar gain

• when solar gain is to be used to offset conditions that are too cold for comfort:

- maximize building exposure and openings facing south (facing north in the southern hemisphere)

- increase thermal mass and envelope insulation

- use dark-colored building exteriors to absorb solar radiation and promote heat gain

*Wind:*

• Wind is a liability in cold climates because it strips heat away; wind can also decrease comfort in hot dry climates when it causes the human body to dehydrate and then overheat;

• wind can be an asset in hot, humid climates to provide natural ventilation:

- use natural ventilation wherever feasible; limit air-conditioning to areas requiring special humidity or temperature control such as artifact storage and computer rooms

- control exposure to wind through plan orientation and configuration, number and position of wall and roof openings and relationship to grade and vegetation

- use wind scoops, thermal chimneys or wind turbines to induce ventilation on sites with limited wind

*Moisture:*

• Moisture can be a liability in the form of humidity, preventing cooling by perspiring in summer. Strategies to reduce the discomfort of high humidity include maximizing ventilation, inducing air flow around facilities and venting or moving moisture-producing functions such as kitchens and shower rooms to outside areas;

• moisture can be an asset by evaporating in hot, dry climates to cool and humidify the air (a natural air-conditioning). Techniques for evaporative cooling include placing facilities where breezes will pass over water features before reaching the buildings, and providing fountains, pools and plants.

*Other Climatic Considerations:*

• Rainfall can be a liability if concentrated runoff from developed surfaces is not managed to avoid erosion;

• rainfall can be an asset if it is collected from roofs for use as drinking water;

• storms, hurricanes, monsoons, typhoons:

- provide or make arrangements for emergency storm shelters

- avoid development in flood plain and storm surge areas

- consider wind effects on walls and roofs

- provide storm shutters for openings

- use appropriate wind bracing and tie-downs

- design facilities to be light and replaceable to be safely sacrificial to large storms, or of sufficient mass and detail to prevent loss of life and material

**Vegetation:**
• Locate and size facilities to avoid cutting mature vegetation and to minimize disruption to, or disassociation with, other natural features;

• use natural vegetation and adjustments in building plan to diminish the visual impact of facilities and to minimize imposition on environmental context;

• in warmer climates, strengthen interplay of facilities with their site environment through minimizing solid walls, creating outdoor activity spaces, etc.

**Topography:**
• Consider building/land interface to minimize disturbance to site character, skyline, vegetation, hydrology and soils;

• consolidate functions or segment facilities to reduce footprint of individual structures to allow sensitive placement within existing landforms;

• use landforms and the sensitive arrangement of buildings to

- diminish the visual impact of facilities

- enhance visual quality by creating a rhythm of open spaces and framed views

- orient visitors to building entrances

- accentuate key landmarks, vistas and facilities

**Water Bodies:**
• Capture views and consider advantages/disadvantages of off-water breezes;

• safeguard water from pollutants from the development and its users;

• minimize visual impact of development on waterfront zones; also consider views from water back to shoreline)

- use building setbacks/buffer zones

- consider building orientation and materials
- avoid light pollution

**Hydrology:**
• Locate and design facilities to minimize erosion and impacts on natural hydrological systems;

• safeguard hydrological system from contamination by development/activities;

• allow precipitation to recharge groundwater naturally, where possible.

**Geology/Soils:**
• Minimize excavation and disturbance to groundcover;

• minimize erosion by avoiding large impervious surface areas and footprints that collect rain and create concentrated runoff onto site.

**Seismic:**
• Determine soil substrate and potential seismic risk;

• use shear walls and appropriate building anchorage and bracing details.

**Pests:**
• Design facilities to minimize intrusion by noxious insects, reptiles and rodents; ensure that facility operators use natural means for pest control.

**Wildlife:**
• Respect importance of biodiversity and the humble role of humans in design;

• avoid disruption of wildlife travel or nesting patterns by sensitive siting of development and by limits set on construction activity and facility operation;

• allow opportunities for users to be aware of indigenous wildlife (observe, but not disturb).

## Human Factors

### Cultural Resources

#### Archaeological resources:
• Use preservation and interpretation of archaeological features for insight into previous cultural responses to the environment, their successes as well as failures.

*Vernacular architecture:*
- Analyze local historic building styles, systems and materials for time-tested approaches in harmony with natural systems;
- use local building material, craftsmen and techniques as much as possible in the development of new facilities.

*Historic resources:*
- Reuse historic buildings whenever possible to assist in their preservation, contribute to the special quality of the place and extend the payback of their embodied energy and materials.

*Anthropology, ethnic background, religion, sociology:*
- Understand the local culture and the need to avoid introduction of socially unacceptable or morally offensive practices;
- consult with local indigenous population for design input as well as to foster a sense of ownership and acceptance;
- include local construction techniques, materials, and cultural considerations (that are environmentally sound) in the development of new facilities.

*Arts and crafts:*
- Incorporate local expressions of art, handiwork, detailing and, when appropriate, technology into new facility design and interior design;
- provide opportunities and space for demonstration of local crafts and performing arts.

**Sensory Experience:**

*Sight:*
- Provide visitors with ready access to educational materials to enhance their understanding and appreciation of the local environment and the threats to it;
- incorporate views of natural and cultural resources into even routine activities to provide opportunities for contemplation, relaxation and appreciation;
- use design principles of scale, rhythm, proportion, balance and composition to enhance the complementary integration of facilities into the environmental context;

- provide visual surprises within design of facilities to stimulate the educational experience;
- limit height of development to below top of tree canopy to preserve visual quality of natural and cultural landscape;
- use muted colors to blend facilities with natural context, unless contradictory to other environmental considerations (reflection/ absorption) or cultural values (customs/taboos).

*Sound:*
- Locate service and maintenance functions away from public areas;
- space lodging units and interpretive stops so that natural, not human, sounds dominate;
- use vegetation to create sound baffle between public and private activities;
- orient openings toward natural sounds such the lapping of waves, babbling of streams and rustling of leaves;
- restrict the use or audio level of unnatural sounds such as radios and televisions.

*Touch:*
- Allow visitors to touch and be in touch with the natural and cultural resources of the site;
- vary walking surfaces to identify or give different quality to different spaces;
- use contrasting textures to direct attention to interpretive opportunities.

*Smell:*
- Allow natural fragrances of vegetation to be enjoyed;
- direct air exhausted from utility areas away from public areas.

*Taste:*
- Provide opportunities to sample local produce and cuisine.

## Environmentally Sensitive Building Materials

### Cradle-to-Grave Analysis

The complete life-cycle energy, environmental and waste implications of each building material must be examined. This cradle-to-grave analysis is the tracing of a material or product and its by-products from its initial source availability and extraction through refinement, fabrication, treatment and additives, and its transportation, use and eventual reuse or disposal. This tracing includes the tabulation of energy consumed and the environmental impacts of each action and material.

- Source of raw ingredients: renewable? sustainable? locally available? nontoxic?

- raw material extraction: energy input? habitat destruction? topsoil erosion? siltation/pollution from runoff?

- transportation: most local source? fuel consumption? air pollution?

- processing and/or manufacturing: energy input? air/water/noise pollution? waste generation and disposal?

- treatments and additives: use of petrochemicals? exposure to, and disposal of, hazardous materials?

- use and operation: energy requirements? longevity of products used? indoor air quality? waste generation?

- resource recovery/disposal: potential for recycling/reusing materials? disposal of solid/toxic wastes?

Two of the best sources for information on the cradle-to-grave implications of commonly used building materials are the American Institute of Architects' *Environmental Resource Guides* (1992-present) and the National Park Service's *Environmentally Responsible Building Product Guide* (1992). To record and tabulate positive and negative environmental actions, report cards should be kept for each material or product in a development. The selection of materials for a sustainable design is then a matter of evaluating the report cards for the lowest total environmental loss.

### Selection Priorities

When the source is sustainable:

- Natural materials are less energy-intensive and polluting to produce, and contribute less to indoor air pollution;

- local materials have a reduced level of energy cost and air pollution associated with their transportation, and can help sustain the local economy;

- durable materials can save on energy costs for maintenance as well as for the production and installation of replacement products.

In selecting building materials, it is helpful to prioritize them by origin, avoiding materials from nonrenewable sources.

*Primary* - materials found in nature such as stone, earth, flora (hemp, jute, reed, cotton), wool and wood:

- Ensure new lumber is from certified sustainably managed forests or certified naturally felled trees;

- use caution that any associated treatments, additives or adhesives do not contain toxins or off-gas volatile organic compounds that contribute to indoor air/atmospheric pollution.

*Secondary* - materials made from recycled products such as wood, aluminum, cellulose, and plastics:

- Verify that production of material does not involve high levels of energy, pollution or waste;

- verify functional efficiency and environmental safety of salvage (reused) materials and products from old buildings;

- look closely at the composition of recycled products – toxins may still be present;

- consider cellulose insulation – it is fireproof and provides a greater R-value per inch thickness than fiberglass;

- specify aluminum from recycled material – it uses 80% less energy to produce over initial production;

- evaluate products containing recycled hydrocarbon-based products – they may help keep used plastics out of landfills but may do little to reduce production and use of plastic from virgin resources;

- keep alert for new developments – new environmentally sound materials from recycled goods are coming on the market every week.

**Tertiary** - man-made materials (artificial, synthetic, non-renewable) having varying degrees of environmental impact such as plywood, plastics and aluminum:

- Avoid use of materials and products containing or produced with chlorofluorocarbons or hydrochlorofluorocarbons that deteriorate the ozone layer;

- avoid materials that off-gas volatile organic compounds, contributing to indoor air/atmospheric pollution;

- minimize use of products made from new aluminum or other materials that are resource-disruptive during extraction and a high energy consumer during refinement.

### Acknowledgement

The Ecotourism Society would like to acknowledge the U.S. National Park Service for allowing reproduction of this chapter from the book, *Guiding Principles of Sustainable Design*, which is now out of print.

# The Role of Landscape in Sustainable Site Design

*By Susan Everett*

## A Working Definition of Sustainable Design

The term "sustainable design," when applied to a site, can be misleading. A full assessment of the sustainability of specific sites would have to take into account regional land planning, appropriate site selection and, finally, site planning and design.

Consider the following conjectural illustration: A tourist lodge is built along a road running parallel to a beach. The lodge is also adjacent to a turtle nesting area. It is possible, within the boundaries of the site, to confine most impacts to the site, to use energy efficiently, to take advantage of renewable energy resources, and to design sensitively and with minimum impact to the site; however, if this development encourages spin-off development along the road, eventually damaging or eradicating the turtle nesting area, it would be a mistake to label this hypothetical development "sustainable."

While this example is overly simplistic, it does demonstrate that sustainable development and ecotourism planning, in particular, must be done at all applicable scales – regional, ecosystem, community and site – and that the decisions made during planning and site selection have equal or greater potential to provide environmental protection than do design and management of individual parcels of land.

Regional assessment and planning can foster the best use of land based on environmental considerations, as well as ensuring that tourism development is feasible before it takes place. ("If you build it they will come" does not apply to tourism – some areas will not support tourism). Such assessment can identify natural and cultural resources that must be protected, as well as potential areas for development, resulting in the designation of various use zones that allow for regional needs to be met, while a site's most valuable assets are protected. Regional assessment and planning provides one of the best tools for natural and cultural resource protection.

Site selection, based on a regional assessment, can assist in finding alternatives to developing protected areas or unspoiled wilderness – a scheme that should be avoided – by identifying potential sites near existing infrastructure, "no-build" options such as adaptive reuse of cultural sites or communities with the potential for "home-stays," where tourists stay in the homes of villagers for a fee. Perhaps most important, site selection processes can assist in developing scenarios to model the unintended consequences of development of potential sites in order to avoid spin-off development that would have negative impacts.

That said, the potential of specific sites to offer examples of environmental responsibility is both great and largely untapped. Solutions to global environmental issues ranging from biodiversity to clean water may be demonstrated in microcosm at the site level. Land use on small and seemingly insignificant sites can have a large cumulative impact. Specific sites can also create a "sense of place" that reflects local history, culture and environment.

## Incorporating Ecotourism Values through Planning, Site Selection and Design

Using the broader definition of sustainable site design that includes regional assessment and planning, site selection processes and site design, the following are objectives that represent core values of ecotourism.

### Protect and Conserve Unspoiled Wilderness and Natural Areas.

According to World Resources 1992-93, 74% of the earth's land is in human use and only the remaining 26% is wilderness, much of it in inaccessible areas. A top priority of ecotourism planning should be the identification and conservation of wilderness, as well as relatively undisturbed natural areas. It is important that what remains of wilderness be conserved and protected, because it cannot be restored. Avoid developing in protected areas or in wilderness unless development is the only means for their ultimate protection. Restrict use of these areas to temporary, removable or low-impact activities.

Consider perimeter areas adjacent to natural or protected areas as potential development sites, select sites that are near existing infrastructure to avoid creating new infrastructure and/or select disturbed sites that would be improved by a sensitive combination of development and restoration.

Ensure that the scale and type of tourism development and activities are in proportion to the carrying capacity of both the ecosystem and the community. Overuse of an area by tourists will mar the resource as

well as the experience of tourism, resulting in the decline of tourism.

### Restore and Regenerate Disturbed Landscapes.

Rather than developing unspoiled areas, restore degraded sites wherever possible. According to *Smithsonian* magazine, "We can now come closer than ever before to restoring the original, natural ecosystems on land that have been trashed. This country – and the world – has no lack of land that has been strip-mined, farm fields that have been exhausted, forests that have been clear-cut, marshes that have been filled. Once we start to restore, we are no longer retreating, trying only to slow the wave of destruction. We begin to actually advance, to regain lost ground."

The advantage of selecting a site that is either disturbed or degraded is that its natural systems and functions can be improved or restored (although not to a pristine condition). Streambank stabilization, stream renewal and restoration, forest regeneration or prairie restoration are some examples of the types of work that specific sites can suggest. In general, use the integration of science, planning, engineering and design principles to restore ecosystem functions, always keeping in mind that restoration is a last resort, not a substitute for preservation.

### Provide Links to the Surrounding Landscape and Community.

Create links between the lodge, nearby sites of cultural and historical interest, neighboring communities and natural features in the vicinity. During site selection, anticipate the consequences of the development of a potential site for its impact on the community, anticipating and avoiding negative effects and fostering beneficial impacts, as defined by the community.

Master planning (particularly on large land holdings), adjacent land uses, public transportation to local communities, pedestrian paths and wildlife connectors are only some of the elements that should be part of a broader approach to site design.

### Identify, Preserve, Protect or Restore or Reuse Cultural and Historic Landscapes and Structures.

Identify and zone or otherwise protect the unique and significant, and look for ways to integrate these resources into the tourist experience. Consider reuse of cultural and historic structures for tourist facilities when it is a viable and acceptable means of saving or restoring less significant properties.

### Ensure that Site Design Contributes to Environmental and Cultural Interpretation.

Create a narrative landscape that reveals history, culture and ecology and supports the values of ecotourism. The visitor experience should be based on interaction and sensory exposure. Look for innovative ways to bring people in contact with nature and wildlife in a meaningful way, while avoiding disruption to the landscape and wildlife. Animal viewing areas, canopy walkways, trails, interpretive centers, guided tours, demonstrations of local culture (both performing and visual arts), environmental interpretative signage and educational materials are only some examples.

### Minimize and Mitigate Building and Human Impacts.

Energy-conserving site design can mitigate the energy use of structures for heating or cooling. Locating windbreaks to divert cold northerly winds, creating wind tunnels to channel cooling breezes to public open spaces or providing shade in hot climates, or planning solar access in the siting of the building to reduce energy requirements are examples of the approaches that can be taken.

Reduce the use of automobiles, when possible, and minimize their penetration into the site. Where roadways are essential, site them sensitively, minimize paving and divert runoff from sensitive areas.

Capture water for reuse or to recharge groundwater by grading to create detention/retention areas. Recycle organic material, such as kitchen waste and wastewater, in the landscape.

### Maintain, Conserve, or Reestablish Biological Systems and Functions.

This approach would look at landscape not as a surface requiring decoration and maintenance but as a natural system. Site design would arise from the site, its ecosystem and cultural context, rather than being imposed on it. The key to creating site sustainability could be summed up by the statement "Strive to main-

tain, conserve or reestablish the integrity and diversity of biological systems and their functions."

Encourage the creation of landscapes which require management, not maintenance. This approach would set closed systems rather than mitigation as the highest goal. There is no reason to assume, for example, that fertilizer and pesticides are necessary, and therefore need to be reduced. Simply avoid fertilizer and pesticide use altogether.

Use living systems, rather than artificial systems that require maintenance and extend development into landscapes. Use living components rather than products when possible. An example of this approach might use soil bioengineering techniques rather than concrete or riprap to stabilize a streambank.

Use tilling and aeration to improve compacted soil; add manures and compost to strengthen the soil and related soil organisms rather than using fertilizer.

Design landscapes to preclude (at best) or to minimize the use of motorized equipment, particularly fossil fuel burning equipment.

Design to minimize the need for construction and site disturbance. For example, creating a site design that works with the existing grade would result in minimizing earthwork, which would have greater positive benefit than the mitigation (e.g., sediment and erosion control) of major grade changes and could preclude the need for hauling in soil or exporting excess soil.

Reduce the area of paved surfaces and use permeable paving to assist in groundwater recharge and preventing runoff. A landscape designed to be compatible with the site conditions, once established, would not need supplemental irrigation (unless the irrigation system was used to distribute wastewater). Many landscapes, once established, are "self-mulching" and would not require removal of green material, only to be replaced by commercial mulch, much of which is shipped from remote locations. Noise and light should also be part of a checklist when looking at both energy use and "pollution."

### Use Indigenous Plants, Soils and Materials.

In restoring disturbed sites or supplementing existing vegetation, set as the highest goal the use of native plants from sustainable sources; protect, conserve and regenerate existing native plant communities. The use of native species for their adaptation to the ecosystem and the region is one reason for their use; however, just as important is the idea of maintaining or creating a "sense of place."

In using native plants, it is important to emphasize plant *communities* rather than individual native plants. Some native plants grow in groves; however, most natives are found in conjunction with other species and the relationships between species should be a consideration in replanting. Site conditions should determine the native plant communities that best fit the conditions of specific areas of a site – low-lying wet areas, rocky slopes facing the south, or shady, dry areas.

It is also essential to restore function as well as species. Landscape "style" (at least in the United States) currently favors planting of specimen trees underlain with low-growing groundcovers. By contrast, a healthy forest ecosystem would contain layers of plants at different stages of maturity competing with and replacing one another as conditions change, and providing habitat for various species of fauna. Using native species to recreate a single layer of same age-same species trees would not restore function, provide habitat or regenerate the landscape.

This is not to say that existing non-native vegetation should be arbitrarily removed from the site. Exotic plants may have value in the landscape; each site should be evaluated and non-native vegetation should be appraised for its value and, when possible, incorporated into new plans. Just as important, identify and remove invasive species, and avoid introducing invasive species onto the site.

Use materials that are on-site or use local materials, when feasible. While it is more environmentally benign to minimize the need for grading by precluding or balancing cut and fill through site design, when fill is required local soil should be used. (This would also make sense in providing an environment where native plants would thrive; the value of planting native plants in imported soil is questionable.) The same would be true for stone, lumber and other materials and products.

### Create a Positive Visitor Experience.

A key challenge of public acceptance of a sustainable site design model will be in creating facilities that also accommodate visitors' needs, provide a rich, meaningful visitor experience and satisfy their desire for beauty. According to Clare Gunn, FASLA, a landscape architect best known for his concepts on balancing tourism development with resource protection, "the real tourism product is the visitor's experience."

Visitors must experience a sense of welcome, hospitality, safety, orientation, privacy, comfort and security consistent with the type of tourist experience being marketed. Without trying to further traditional notions that guest facilities should have all the comforts of home, even the most rustic of elements can be well designed, beautifully crafted and functional, and even the simplest of settings can provide a sense of orientation, welcome and hospitality. Tourists also prize beauty and expect that tourism development will take advantage of views and vistas, and that the facilities themselves will be handsome. It is not enough that nearby natural areas are beautiful; man-made additions to the landscape should also be attractive out of respect for the natural surroundings and the visitor. The use of solid principles of planning and design are essential to these goals.

In order for sustainable development to gain public acceptance, the highest levels of creativity should be used to develop a new aesthetic for tourist facilities and sites (as opposed to the existing aesthetic of multi-story buildings, circular drives, swimming pools, fountains, clipped hedges and turf) and for enriching the experience and understanding of natural landscapes, while incorporating all the other values of ecotourism.

### Use a Holistic Approach to Sustainable Site Design.

The previous objectives mention many varying elements that must be taken into consideration when developing tourist facilities. These elements are best approached through holistic, integrative processes rather than individually. Site design should synthesize considerations of:

1. environmental elements (hydrology, climate),

2. human factors (local culture, historic site uses, the client's plan),

3. context (adjacent land use, neighboring communities),

4. sustainability issues (energy efficiency, environmental sensitivity), and

5. special issues (such as hazard mitigation in fire-prone areas).

Each of these factors may influence seemingly unrelated decisions. For example, a decision to seek energy-efficient technology in a climate that has a high rate of solar exposure might indicate roof-mounted solar panels as a solution. Add the element of a historic site with ancient buildings, however, and what was formerly seen as a solution would be ruled out in order to maintain the historic integrity of the site and its buildings.

## Ecotourism as a Frontier of Sustainable Development

As the first "market" that has espoused the concepts of sustainable development in facility design, ecotourism may provide one of the most effective means for demonstrating to large numbers of people that sustainable design is as desirable as – or more desirable than – typical unsustainable models. The ultimate value of sustainable tourism facilities may be in the example they set, and their success may be measured by the degree of adoption as a standard for development for more typical tourism and for purposes other than tourism.

Because there are so few models of sustainable design and development, the ecotourism market should do more than mimic typical development with a few minor changes. Rather it should take the lead in creating models that radically overhaul existing prototypes. This would mean that ecotourism developers, planners and designers would strive for the most value and greatest positive impact, rather than making minor changes that would allow them to use a "green" label. For example, rather than specifying a manufactured product that uses recycled materials and shipping it from a remote location, specify an indigenous product from a sustainable source. When no sustainable source can be located, examine the feasibility and potential benefits of creating a sustainable source, an action that could simultaneously create local economic opportunities.

In seeking the highest value, prevention of negative impacts such as pollution would be given a higher priority than mitigation. Developers would commit to following existing regional plans or advocating plan creation before developing. Site selection would consider not just availability, price and convenience, but also the impacts on nearby communities and the ecosystem, and the potential for spin-off development – both positive and negative.

And because every site is unique, the resulting design should likewise be unique, reflecting the local environment, culture and history, as well as the target market, rather than "knocking-off" what has come to be typical.

These efforts will require inventiveness, creativity and broad participation – both professional interdisciplinary collaboration and community involvement. Their success will depend, first and foremost, on a high level of tourist satisfaction. Environmental, economic and community sustainability – all important and intrinsic to ecotourism – must foster, not displace, a positive and rewarding tourist experience which, in the final analysis, is the ultimate test of sustainability.

### Literature cited:

World Resources. 1992-93. *Table 17.1 Land Area and Use. 1978-89.* Sources: Food and Agriculture Organization of the United Nations, Eurostat, United Nations Population Division and J. M. McCloskey and H. Spalding.

Wiley, John P., Jr. "Phenomena, comment and notes," *Smithsonian* 19 (12); pp. 32 ff.

Reynolds, John, Frederick Steiner, Carol Franklin, John Lyle, Peter Jacobs, Susan Everett. 1993. *Declaration on Environment and Development.* American Society of Landscape Architects.

Gunn, Clare A. 1991. "Redefining the Tourism Product: The Environmental Experience," Session presented at Travel and Tourism Research Association Conference, June 9-13, 1991.

# To Power Ecotourism Facilities

*By Elizabeth H. Richards*

## Introduction

Renewable energy technologies are increasingly becoming the power sources of choice for a wide variety of applications throughout the world. Whether the need is for lighting, water supplies, communications, heating, refrigeration, irrigation, rural electrification or even large-scale power generation, renewables are establishing themselves as the least-cost and most reliable source of energy in a growing number of situations. Renewable energy sources also usually have less impact on the environment than traditional alternatives. As the market for these technologies has expanded, the products have improved and their prices have declined, so that they are now used routinely in many residential, commercial, industrial and utility applications. The future portends continued growth of this industry, especially as the issue of sustainability receives increasing attention.

Ecotourism and renewable energy are natural partners. From an ecological perspective, renewables are an appropriate choice due to their minimal environmental impact. In addition, renewable energy resources (e.g., sunshine and wind) typically are abundant at ecotourism destinations, and the remoteness of many ecotourism sites makes renewable energy an economically attractive choice as well. The amount of energy required by an ecotourism facility is compatible with what renewable energy systems can supply, and the level of local infrastructure required for successful operation of an ecotourism facility is consistent with that required for renewable energy systems. Furthermore, renewable energy systems offer the type of alternative experience that ecotourism clientele are seeking.

## What is Renewable Energy?

Renewable energy is defined here as the collection of energy resources that are replenished at least as fast as they are used or that are available in such sufficient quantities that their use does not significantly deplete their supply. These include solar and wind energy, hydropower, geothermal energy and biomass. Non-renewable energy resources are those that are used more quickly than they are replaced, such as oil, coal and other fossil fuels.

## Renewable Energy Technologies Appropriate for Ecotourism Facilities

A variety of renewable energy technologies make sense for ecotourism facilities. Generally, small independent ("stand-alone") systems are most appropriate and most common. However, powering a large facility, even a village, with renewables is possible and has been done, usually using wind or a hybrid combination of wind and another energy source. Solar and wind systems are the most likely renewable resources for an ecotourism facility, although micro-hydro systems may make sense where there is sufficient flowing water, and geothermal systems may be appropriate where such a resource exists – hot springs are an obvious example. Biomass is another renewable resource, although until recently only large systems (power-plant size) were commercially available. Generally, the environmental effects of using renewable energy systems are considered to be relatively minimal compared to more traditional alternatives, but they vary both with technology and application, and each situation must be evaluated on its own characteristics.

### Solar Thermal Technologies

Solar thermal technologies are probably the most widely known renewable technology. Solar water heating, for example, is a familiar sight in many parts of both the developed and developing worlds. Solar ovens are also becoming more popular, and though they may require some adjustments in cooking or meal routines to maximize their effectiveness, they earn rave reviews for the quality of meals they can cook as well as their potential for offsetting the burning of wood or other cooking fuels. Solar industrial-process-heat systems are available for applications such as laundry facilities, and solar stills for desalinating water and ice makers powered with solar thermal energy are also entering the marketplace. In addition to the above technologies, which all make direct use of the heat energy from the sun, there are also technologies that convert the sun's thermal energy into electricity. Although most of these are best suited for large systems producing bulk power, dish-Stirling systems, which use a parabolic dish reflector to focus sunlight onto a Stirling engine, are now becoming commercial-

ly available and have possibilities for smaller, stand-alone systems.

### Photovoltaics

Photovoltaics, or PV, is an increasingly well known technology as well. PV modules have no moving parts and use semiconductor technology to convert sunlight directly into electricity. PV systems produce electricity that can be used for virtually any purpose. Photovoltaics is especially well suited for water pumping because water can be pumped during daylight hours, stored in a tank and then gravity-fed when it is needed. Lighting is another common use of photovoltaics, although batteries are necessary for use at night as is the case for most other applications unless they are needed only during daylight hours. Other popular uses of photovoltaics include communications, residential and remote facility power and remote monitoring. Photovoltaic technology is currently most economical for situations where there is no access to an existing electrical grid, which makes it very suitable for a wide range of ecotourism facilities. New PV technologies, such as water disinfection, are entering the marketplace and show promise for ecotourism as well.

### Solar Building Technologies

Many solar building technologies are appropriate for ecotourism facilities, starting with energy efficiency. Careful attention to designing suitable buildings can have a dramatic effect on energy needs and costs. For example, in many climates, proper building design and siting combined with the use of natural ventilation, shade and fans eliminate the need for air conditioning even in areas where recent development practices would appear to indicate otherwise. In colder climates, sufficient insulation greatly reduces heating requirements and their associated environmental costs; solar-heated buildings may eliminate them altogether. In climates with sufficient variations in temperature, incorporating thermal mass into buildings can increase comfort levels without increasing energy requirements. Incorporating day-lighting (the use of natural light) into a building can also result in significant energy savings and frequently results in a more pleasant space as well. New architectural designs and emerging technologies (such as PV roof tiles) are also increasingly allowing the integration of renewable energy systems into the buildings themselves.

## Wind Energy

In areas where sufficient wind resource exists, wind technologies frequently are the most economical choice for meeting many energy needs. Mechanical windmills, used primarily to pump water, have long been a familiar sight around the world. Now wind-electric technologies are used in a wide variety of applications, ranging from small turbines used to keep small boats' batteries charged to huge wind farms providing bulk power to electrical grids. Technologies suitable for ecotourism applications include small (100s of watts) turbines used to power individual cabins as well as medium (1 to 10 kilowatts) turbines used to power a larger ecolodge facility. In areas where there is sufficient wind, wind-electric technologies may currently be the most cost-effective energy supply choice for making ice because of the relatively large power requirements for this application. Like photovoltaics, wind-electric systems generally require the use of batteries to allow full-time operation. In areas where the wind resource is seasonal, wind systems are combined with other energy sources, such as PV and/or fossil fuel generators, to ensure year-round availability.

## Small-scale Hydropower

Hydropower is generally associated with large dams and bulk power generation. However, in areas where an appropriate resource exists, small-scale hydropower (also known as micro-hydropower) systems have proven to be a reliable and economic means of generating electricity with minimal environmental impact. Micro-hydropower systems exist in several forms. One approach is simply a small version of a traditional dam, although the environmental effects of this approach may be prohibitive. A variation on this involves putting a dam on a side channel created to divert a portion of the water flow. Where a sufficient natural elevation drop exists, a third approach can be used where a small side channel is created to divert a portion of the water directly through a turbine with no dam. A fourth approach requires no alteration of the stream flow or banks and involves a turbine that is placed directly in the water flow. Depending on the resource available and what environmental concerns are present, some ecotourism facilities may be able to meet all or part of their energy needs with small-scale hydropower.

## Other Renewable Energy Technologies

Several other renewable energy technologies may have appropriate applications for ecotourism facilities, although their use in such situations is not as well established as the technologies described above. In addition to the natural hot springs popular with many tourists in various places around the world, where the appropriate resource exists, small geothermal systems can be used for both heating and cooling of buildings and the production of electricity. A variety of biomass technologies are gaining increasing acceptance and use around the world, although their use in ecotourism applications is not established. Various ocean energy technologies are under development around the world as well, but they are not yet field-proven or commercially available.

## Advantages and Limitations of Renewable Energy

Renewable energy systems can successfully provide power for a myriad of applications. However, they may not be the best answer to every power need. It is important to consider both the advantages and limitations of the various options before selecting a power source. Experience has shown that unrealistic expectations of what a renewable energy system can supply, and at what cost, lead to dissatisfaction and failed installations.

• Although renewable energy systems make use of renewable resources, they are generally resource-dependent. Which technology is appropriate at a given site is dependent on what the available renewable energy resources are. In addition, the outputs of solar, wind and sometimes hydro systems are affected by the weather. Furthermore, although resources such as sunshine and wind are free, renewable energy systems can deliver only a set amount of power (unlike a conventional electrical grid, which delivers relatively unlimited power on demand), and it is very important to design the systems using accurate assessments of the loads.

- On a life-cycle cost basis, renewable energy systems are frequently the most economical and cost-effective choice for supplying energy for many applications. However, many renewable energy technologies have high initial costs, which can make them less affordable than the traditional alternatives.

- Many renewable energy systems can be sized for any desired amount of power, and many systems are modular so that they can be expanded as needs dictate. However, the type of power produced by some of the technologies (direct current from photovoltaics, for example) is not necessarily optimum in all cases and may have to be converted.

- Many renewable energy technologies require much lower levels of maintenance than the traditional alternatives. However, "low maintenance" does not mean "no maintenance," and some level of local infrastructure is required to ensure adequate system care and spare parts.

- Renewable energy resources are generally considered to have minimal environmental impact. In general, their impact is less than that of fossil fuels, but the environmental effects of renewable energy can be significant and should not be overlooked.

## Economics of Renewable Energy

Some renewable energy technologies have a reputation for high cost – photovoltaics in particular. When compared against conventional grid electricity in the United States, photovoltaically generated electricity is indeed three or four times as expensive. On the other hand, electricity generated by large wind turbines in a good wind regime is cost-competitive. However, in many locations throughout the world, including many ecotourism destinations, grid electricity is not available, so the economics become more a question of

value in delivering an end use or service rather than relative prices of energy. When grid electricity is not available or even when a grid is available but an extension is necessary, photovoltaics is frequently the most cost-effective choice for small energy needs (10 to 500 watts), depending on import duties for the technology, despite its relatively high cost per kilowatt-hour. In areas with good wind resource, wind power is frequently the most cost-effective choice, especially for medium-sized energy needs (1 to 10 kilowatts).

Since the purchase price of an energy system, renewable or not, is only part of the overall cost of the system, life-cycle cost analyses must be used to make accurate comparisons of various energy-supply alternatives. The following factors should be included: Fuel costs, maintenance costs, transportation costs, reliability and externalities such as environmental effects. It is also essential to understand the importance of energy efficiency and conservation. Since renewable energy is often used in high-value applications, it is usually much less expensive to invest first in reducing loads through efficiency and conservation measures rather than increasing the size of the renewable energy system.

## Designing and Procuring Renewable Energy Systems

A number of guides are available to assist with renewable energy system design, and the renewable energy industry can also provide assistance (see Resources, p. 140). The following steps define the basic issues.

The first step in selecting a renewable energy system is to assess what renewable resources are available at the site. Weather data and anecdotal information can be used as indications of solar and wind resources, but actual resource data is preferable if it is available (check with the National Renewable Energy Laboratory; see Resources, p. 140). Wind data in particular is important, as wind varies significantly with altitude, season and local topography.

The next step is to estimate the energy needs, or loads, and the types of energy needed (electricity, heat, mechanical, etc.) including total usage, peak demand, daily load profile and seasonal demand variations. It is important to be realistic, as an undersized system will frustrate its users and an oversized system will waste money.

The third step is to determine the required days of storage, or autonomy, needed for the particular application (for cloudy or windless days, etc.). "Typical" systems in "typical" climates generally include about three days of autonomy, but this is dependent on the criticality of the load. More storage will generally result in higher reliability but will also increase system cost.

The fourth step is to compare the loads and types of energy needed with the available resources to determine what technologies make sense.

After determining the basic system requirements through the steps above, it is appropriate to involve a system supplier to further refine the possibilities. The system supplier can provide more detailed design information and analysis, as well as cost estimates. It is recommended that attention be given to "service after the sale" to ensure continued, long-term system operation. Other factors to consider include environmental impact, safety of the system and protection against theft and vandalism.

# Chapter 3:

# Financing the Ecolodge

# Determining the Economic Feasibility of a Lodging Property

*By Lani Kane*

Most simply put, a project is determined to be "feasible" if its economic value exceeds its development costs by a sufficient ratio to provide a satisfactory investment return. The feasibility study process may be utilized for proposed developments and for existing properties or establishments considering renovation, expansion or repositioning. This paper outlines the steps necessary to complete a feasibility analysis for a typical lodging property. While this generic outline provides a basic overview of the feasibility process, traits specific to each type of product studied should be factored into the analysis. In general, a feasibility study may be separated into two phases: The Market Study and The Cash Flow/Feasibility Analysis.

A market study focuses on understanding the project's existing and future conditions and provides the basis to develop conclusions about market support. Moreover, additional factors integral to the financial analysis (e.g., wage rates, utility costs) are identified. The financial analysis involves understanding the key market and operational factors necessary to estimate a project's potential cash flow stream. In addition, development costs and the appropriate financing structure are researched and determined to provide the basis for calculating the estimated financial return from the project.

Combined, these analyses assist in providing an independent assessment of whether a project is economically sensible. It should be noted, however, that undertaking a feasibility study does not guarantee the success of a development. The process is merely a tool to assist in understanding and planning for a project's initial risks, thereby increasing the comfort level associated with a project.

A flow chart outlining the steps of a feasibility analysis follows on page 52. A sample report outline concludes this overview.

## STEP 1: Project Concept: Definition and Refinement

The key in developing the project concept is to answer the questions:

Is the proposed concept designed to meet the needs of its target markets?

Is the design sustainable?

- Develop project concept with team approach, including feasibility consultants, land planners/environmental consultants and architects; refine concept throughout the study process to provide key characteristics to fill market voids and allow for competitiveness; apply sustainable design test to determine compatibility with local environment and community.

## STEP 2: Site Analysis

The site analysis provides the basis for understanding the attributes of the project's location and its compatibility with the proposed concept, accessibility of potential users, surrounding amenities and facilities and future development trends that may impact the development under study. Generally a professional study of the environmental and soil conditions, as well as availability of utility/infrastructure, should be undertaken. The depth and focus of these studies will vary greatly depending upon the type of lodging and its setting.

- Analyze physical characteristics, including topography, unique attributes and environmental and zoning considerations;

- review location's advantages and disadvantages;

- understand existing and future area developments;

- determine access to general area and project site.

## STEP 3: Market Area Definition and Analysis

The area review provides an understanding of the project's community. This analysis should include eco-

nomic and demographic trends, employment sources, climate and transportation. Social issues such as safety and community support should be explored.

- Define/review area market factors. Check local/outside data sources, such as:
    - U.S. Department of Commerce
    - U.S. Agency for International Development
    - the World Bank
    - local government sources
    - local/regional lending institutions

- research and analyze the economic and demographic factors affecting the primary market, such as:
    - population characteristics
    - employment trends and unemployment rates
    - population and employment projections
    - labor force characteristics
    - tourism and visitation trends
    - housing trends
    - crime
    - local people/customs/culture
    - area attractions/natural attributes

## STEP 4: Competitive Supply Analysis

The supply analysis is an integral component of the market review and provides the basis for determining a project's existing and future competition, advantages and disadvantages and, finally, competitive positioning. A clear understanding of a project's competitive environment allows the proposed project to position itself in the marketplace as a viable competitor.

- Determine comparison criteria for analyzing competitors:

---

### Flow Chart of Steps for Feasibility Analysis

| | | | | | | | |
|---|---|---|---|---|---|---|---|
| Project Concept Defined | ⇨ | Site Analysis | ⇨ | Market Area Economic & Demographic Analysis | ⇨ | Competitive Supply Analysis | ⇨ |
| Demand Analysis | ⇨ | Cash Flow & Economic Analysis | ⇨ | Determination of Project & Land Costs | ⇨ | Financing Considerations & Feasibility Conclusions | |

---

- concept/size
- location
- market captured
- pricing

• review of competitors' key attributes:
- advantages/disadvantages
- utilization/room rates achieved
- accessibility/transportation issues
- affiliation/referral groups
- marketing tactics/consumer profile
- cultural offerings
- development costs

• research new projects being developed that may impact proposed project;

• refine project concept to satisfy market needs.

## STEP 5: Demand Analysis and Utilization

The demand analysis provides the final support in forecasting a proposed project's utilization. This step answers the basic questions:

What sources of demand exist for a project in its anticipated location?

What is the depth of the identified demand?

Are demand sources expected to grow or decline over the analysis period?

Geographically, where is demand expected to originate?

What are the characteristics of the individual demand sources?

What is the project's anticipated ability to capture its fair share of market demand?

What steps/modifications can be made to increase the project's capture?

• Interview travel professionals to understand consumer profiles and needs;

• analyze depth of demand for existing facilities:
- historic travel patterns
- natural source markets
- new source markets
- anticipated growth in demand

• determine proposed project's position in com-petitive marketplace; review alternatives to enhance competitive positioning;

• anticipate capture of demand, or utilization, by proposed project.

## STEP 6: Cash Flow Analysis and Economic Valuation

The cash flow analysis is the first step in the financial phase of the study. This process can be divided into two steps: Cash flow/pro forma analysis and valuation/discounted cash flow.

• Preparation of assumptions for cash flow projections, including:
- length of projection period
- revenues: room, food, beverage, ancillary
- departmental expenses
- effective gross income
- undistributed expenses
- net operating income;
- fixed charges: capital expenditures, taxes, insurance;
- net cash flow

• consider impact of fiscal/development incentives;

• discounted cash flow analysis:
- residual value calculation: A sale of the property is typically assumed to occur at the end of the projection period; anticipated proceeds are determined based upon the fol-lowing year's Net Cash Flow capitalized by an "exit" or "terminal" capitalization rate, less sales/closing costs
- terminal and going in capitalization rate research and determination

• discount rates analysis: The discount rate is a func-tion of rates of return in competing investments, coupled with specific risk profiles of the property being analyzed. The basic premise involves the expectation of receiving the full recovery of the amount invested and a return on the investment commensurate with time value of money and asso-ciated risk factors. Additional factors:
- analysis of historic and anticipated inflation
- tax considerations

- risk factors associated with the uncertainty of the cash flow projections
- illiquidity (the inability to dispose of the property at a reasonable price within a desired time frame)
- management risk (hotels are typically management-intensive compared to other investments)

## STEP 7: Determination of Project Development and Land Costs

This phase of the analysis focuses on the costs of the project during the construction period.

- Infrastructure and land;
  - purchase price
  - environmental studies
  - site preparation
  - landscaping
  - legal costs
- improvements;
  - construction materials
  - interior finishings
- pre-opening costs;
  - design
  - environmental preservation/compatibility
  - permits/fees
  - marketing costs

---

*Suggested Report Outline for Potential Market Demand and Estimated Financial Feasibility of a Proposed Lodging Property*

*Anytown, Florida*
location and climate
history and political characteristics
population, language and currency
economic overview
tourism
transportation
future outlook

*Project Description, Neighborhood and Site Analysis*
project concept
town and neighborhood review
site location and description
sustainability

*Lodging Environment*
comparable lodging supply
supply additions

*Demand Analysis*
consumer profile
future demand
seasonality

*Estimated Future Occupancy and Average Room Rate*
estimated future occupancy
estimated future average room rates

*Estimated Future Operating Results*
inflation assumption
revenue analysis
departmental expenses analysis
undistributed operating expense analysis

*Development Cost Analysis*
land costs
site development costs
building/improvement costs
soft costs

*Feasibility Conclusions*
discounted cash flow analysis
- residual value
- discount rates/investment yields
financing structure
conclusions

*Appendices*
maps
economic indicators
tourist arrivals
comparable lodging facilities
estimated future performance/pro forma

- operating capital
- consultants fees

- review for reasonableness vs competitors/industry standards.

## STEP 8: Financing Considerations

Underwriting parameters incorporated into the discounted cash flow analysis is the next step in calculating the financial feasibility of a project.

- Overall capital requirements;

- lending parameters: A loan-to-value ratio (LTV) is calculated by dividing the loan amount by the value of the property; maximum LTVs for ecolodges and small properties located in developing regions currently range from 60 to 70%. A debt service coverage ratio is the relationship between a project's anticipated net operating income and its annual debt service; a minimum debt service coverage ratio of 1.4 to 1.7 is typically required.

## STEP 9: Feasability Conclusion

Based on results of Steps 6, 7 and 8, review implications of the proposed project, debt and equity requirements and projected financial returns to gauge "feasibility."

In conclusion, a feasibility study is a useful tool to provide input before development. The process is most successful when combined with the development of a detailed marketing and promotional strategy. A feasibility study is based on experience, judgment and understanding of the local market coupled with the project's anticipated positioning and acceptance in the marketplace. As such, while the process is not infallible, it can provide a greater understanding of some of the risks associated with development. Moreover, the results of the study can provide feedback about conceptual modifications, marketing tactics or profitability initiatives to strengthen the overall project and to assist in a smoother development process.

# Ecolodge Finance and Investment Strategies

*By Donald E. Hawkins*

Considerable attention has been given worldwide to the role of ecotourism in supporting conservation and generating new funds for resource protection and management. Ecotourism is a catalyst for job creation and enterprise development which can provide direct economic benefits to local people living in or near natural areas that attract domestic and international tourists. Little attention has been given to the careful examination of financial mechanisms and resources that can be used at the local level to fund ecotourism projects. This paper will be concerned with the expansion of funding of ecotourism projects by linking project developers with local and international public and private financial resources, including multilateral and bilateral sources of assistance and funds.

The proliferation of ecotourism projects is viewed by some skeptics as a desperate and unrealistic attempt to resolve the intractable problem of revenue generation for conservation and protected area management. The greatest challenge in the design of these ecotourism projects in often remote and fragile areas of high biodiversity is that of scale. The project must be viable financially and must generate sufficient revenues to offset the costs of protecting the asset, but must be small enough to attract only sufficient tourists whose presence, at any one time, will not destroy the assets they have come to view.

An equally important issue is the compensation or other incentives that will induce the local population to preserve, rather than use up, their natural assets, which often constitute the main source of their livelihood. Skeptics argue that the long-term change in behavior cannot be accomplished within the much shorter time frame of the project; hence the pressure to find long-term financing for implementation of the project in perpetuity, with some advocating sustainable ecotourism projects.

In March 1993, The Ecotourism Society Funding Policy Committee convened a meeting at the Interamerican Investment Bank to explore funding options for ecotourism developers, with particular attention given to Latin America (Roldán, 1993). The purpose of that meeting was to provide an opportunity for developers of low-impact tourism projects, with experience in Latin America, to discuss the problems and opportunities they face in obtaining finance and to share concerns with representatives of the international finance community. Developers working in Belize, Cuba, Venezuela and Ecuador participated. Representatives of the Interamerican Investment Bank, the Interamerican Development Bank, the International Finance Corporation, the Global Environment Fund, the Overseas Private Investment Corporation and the Agency for International Development discussed their programs. One private bank from Ecuador, the Banco del Pinchicha, was represented, as were non-governmental organizations.

Participants were concerned initially with the difficulty of identifying potential funding sources, and how to use capital sources from large private sector financial institutions, bilateral agencies and multilateral institutions. The small size of many ecolodge projects was listed as a major constraint. The participants listed several qualities which distinguish ecotourism development projects from traditional forms of tourism development, outlined below.

## Essential Qualities of Ecotourism Development

*Design:*
- Conformance to sustainable design and development practices;
- inclusion of environmental interpretation programs;
- phased development strategy: i.e., start small and expand gradually.

*Financial:*
- Catalyst for other small-scale micro enterprises;
- prevention of visitor spending leakages in order to increase economic multiplier effects, including conservation-related impacts;
- provision of benefits to local protected areas, including fees to cover management of parks;
- encouragement of government to ensure that some tourism-generated revenues are channeled to park protection and natural area management.

*Environment and Conservation:*
- Impact analyses and design-oriented research to ensure that the facility is developed on an environmentally sound basis;
- ongoing working relationships with conservation-related NGOs;
- commitment to efficient use of resources, including state-of-the-art energy generation and reuse of existing resources through recycling;
- inclusion of planning measures to ensure conservation benefits;
- linkage with local conservation projects, particularly by providing opportunities for tourists to interact with local people or volunteer for conservation-related project activities.

*Cultural and Local Practices:*
- Involvement of local people in ownership and management beyond simply service-level employment;
- encouragement of cultural sensitivity, interpersonal exchanges and avoidance of an "enclave" mentality;
- use of indigenous assets, especially art forms and cultural motifs.

## Problems and Opportunities

While there is a lack of comparables and success indicators in ecolodge case studies, participants were able to identify key issues of funding problems and development opportunities.

*Funding Problems:*
- Macro economic differences between countries;
- unresponsive local financial institutions, and need for new financing mechanisms;
- excessively high local bank loan rates in developing countries;
- bank collateral requirements not responsive to value-added resources provided by parks, particularly in long-term lease concessions;

- lack of working capital, and inadequate funds for marketing and promotion;

- determining the appropriate scale of development, and how to avoid saturation of tourism destinations;

- preventing land speculation;

- balancing low-impact development and long-term conservation goals with shorter-term return on investment and profitability requirements;

- lack of available infrastructure and trained personnel;

- difficulty for some entrepreneurs to meet high standard demands of ecotourism;

- need for consumer education about ecotours and their conservation role;

- limited opportunities for local ownership and management.

*Development Opportunities:*

- Expansion of ecotourism-related microbusiness enterprises;

- availability of micro loans and "incubator" assistance for individuals and small enterprises not eligible for loans and equity investment support;

- existing lines of credit to financial intermediaries and commercial banks in the Latin American region now available for sound ecotourism projects;

- rapid expansion of social equity and emerging market mutual funds that could provide funding for capital market-oriented ecotourism investments;

- likelihood of more widely available funds for feasibility studies through multilateral trade investment and financing sources;

- creation of local and national organizations to deal with ecotourism issues;

- utilization of debt for nature swaps;

- growing demand for environmentally sound tourism, and interest of established tourism industry in the ecotourism market;

- expanding network of facilities and services by inbound ecotour operators;

- mega-tourism complexes that could serve as hubs for ecotourism;

  - acting as base camps in less ecologically sensitive sites

  - revitalizing the mass tourism product

- mass media and special interest publications receptive to providing free editorial content and press coverage.

## Funding Realities

At the ecotourism funding meeting in 1993, representatives of financing agencies provided an overview of their activities, particularly with reference to ecotourism projects. At that time, none of the agencies had focused specifically on programs designed to fund ecotourism projects, except for the Overseas Private Investment Corporation (OPIC). OPIC has been attempting to develop an environmental equity fund which could provide direct funding for ecotourism projects. The International Finance Corporation (IFC) representatives were concerned primarily about "economy of scale" concerns due to the small number of rooms of most ecolodge projects. IFC suggested that ecotourism projects should attempt to affiliate with large multinational corporations in the hospitality business (like Hyatt, Marriott, Sheraton, Club Med, Choice and others) who have experience in project development and finance and can provide essential management and marketing services. It was noted that IFC is also involved in implementing a global environmental facility pilot project, costing US$1 billion per year over a period of three to four years. There may be some possibility of funding ecotourism projects under the biodiversity elements of a GEF Project.

Jorge Roldán, an economist with the Interamerican Investment Corporation (IIC), reported on his study of ecotourism private sector project performance over the past five years. According to Roldán (1993), the most successful ecotourism operations seem to share some of the following characteristics:

- Most ecotourism projects cost less than $5 million;

- they operate on a small scale, and the number of tourists is strictly regulated to avoid over-exploitation of resources and harmful effects on the wildlife;

- the operator often has a monopoly on access to a particular area;

- educational materials – cultural and environmental do's and don'ts – are provided to the visitor;

- advanced training for local staff is ongoing, and local people are fully involved in the project's operation and planning and well compensated in order to make tourism work more attractive;

- a percentage of profits is generally donated to local community projects, ecolodge research, local environmental groups or student scholarships.

Other presentations given by the Interamerican Investment Corporation, Interamerican Development Bank and OPIC made it clear that, although there are potential funds available, costly prefeasibility analyses and project documentation are required in most cases. Ecotourism developers should be familiar with guidelines for project financing usually required by private sector banks and binational-multinational corporations.

## Information on Funding Sources

It is essential to know where funds can be obtained for ecotourism projects from multilateral institutions, bilateral agencies and the private sector. The appendix on page 63 includes a list of financing sources, including selected resources available to Andean, Caribbean and Central American countries.

MIGA has developed a system to manage the investment and promotion process and to coordinate an international network for investment promotion agencies. The system includes an investor tracking system (ITS) and a business operating conditions (BOC) database system. Recently, MIGA has been involved in tourism related investment information and development networking activities focused on the Eastern Caribbean and South American regions, and expects to expand its efforts in other priority areas. (See MIGA Marketing Program for the Tourism Industry on the following page). For further information, contact Martin Hardigan, PAS Administrator, MIGA and Manager, Investment Promotion Special Projects, FIAS,

1818 H St. NW, Room H-6065, Washington, DC 20433, USA. Phone 202-473-0687, Fax 202-676-0512. See chart on the following page.

## Recommendations

The following recommendations resulted directly from the funding policy committee meeting referred to previously, and are consistent with the types of issues addressed throughout this paper.

1. Low-impact development projects might be linked to bring the total dollar value amount requested up to amounts required by international finance institutions. Several representatives from finance institutions also recommended linking small ecotourism facilities with larger hotels (serving as "base camps") to achieve the economy of scale requirements of financing institutions.

   It is possible for a sponsor or consortium to plan two or three developments in different areas of the country as a network. An example of this is the Central America Nature Tourism and Science Network developed in Costa Rica proposed by the Real Estate Investment Overseas Company (RIOC). The proposed Costa Rica Nature Tourist/Science Network would consist of a central resort with several resort stations near national parks and nature preserves.

   The central resort would be a full service destination beach resort. The stations are working farms or ranches, augmented with lodging, restaurant and educational facilities. Guests from the central resort and other tour groups would use these stations to embark on guided nature tours in the parks in groups of six to ten people. Scientific research teams could also make use of these stations. Presently, the RIOC is considering developing the central vacation village on the Pacific coast in Guanacaste with stations in the Santa Rosa National Park, Juan Castro Blanco National Park, Tortuguero National Park, Corcovado National Park and Cano Negro Wildlife Reserve, and the La Amistad International Park, among others.

2. Case studies should be developed which identify the essential qualities and operating characteristics

# MIGA Investment Marketing Program for the Tourism Industry

*Phases of Project Development*

**Phase 1:**

Decision by MIGA member country to define role of tourism industry within overall country strategy for economic development.

**Phase 2:**

Request of MIGA to assist in analysis of tourism as tool for economic development. The request may come from an individual country or regional organization. The basic industry and institutional diagnostic will have a regional focus. The review will include commentary on the following, dependent on country needs: 1) public and private sector institutions/companies shaping the industry; 2) economic development impact; 3) products; 4) markets; 5) competition; 6) potential investors; and 7) activities and resources of international organizations.

**Phase 3:**

If determined that the industry matches country development priorities, MIGA moves ahead with designing a program to develop country strategies to: 1) increase the capacity of the country to develop the industry; and 2) implement an investment promotion strategy for the sector.

The components of the program are as follows:

1) *Strategic Planning Seminar:* To review/create national tourism strategy for integrated development (emphasis on implementation – i.e., best practices review of current/necessary institutional capacity and building public/private partnerships;

2) *Investment Promotion Strategies Workshop:* To review past investment promotion activities and permanent marketing tools (emphasis on harmonization/efficiency – i.e., best practices review of IPAs and utilization/integration of promotional resources);

3) *Project Financing Strategy Seminar/Doing Business with Foreign Partners:* To demystify search for project finance and analyze current projects (emphasis on targeting – i.e., individual project promotion programs);

4) *Market Survey and Reverse Missions:* To review investor attitudes and needs (emphasis on database development – i.e., direct communication with target audience through direct mail, teleresearch and reverse missions to provide vital feedback for projects and overall investment climate);

5) *Investors' Conference:* A practicum/focal point for initial series of activities (dual emphasis on short-term project finance and test of long-term national strategy and permanent marketing vehicles).

**Phase 4:**

One-year follow-up program in two parts: 1) refinement of permanent marketing tools (i.e., CD-Rom, IPA-Net and MiS System); and 2) individual country and subregional investment promotion activities. The process of designing and implementing the individual county and subregional programs repeats the phases and components listed above.

*By Dr. Ken Kwaku, Global Program Manager*
*Multilateral Investment Guarantee Agency (MIGA), World Bank Group*

of a successful ecotourism lodge. Providing comparable financial and management information on successful ecotourism lodges to financial institutions would be an important tool in the setting of standards for ecotourism finance in the future. Profitability and marketability standards will need to be compared with more traditional forms of tourism lodging to determine if the concept of economy of scale is valid in this case. Anecdotal evidence, similar to that offered by developer Stanley Selengut of Maho Bay Camps, seems to suggest that low overhead and efficient use of resources can actually make small ecotourism lodge facilities as profitable as large ones. In addition, Maho Bay's 97% high season occupancy rate suggests that ecotourism resorts may well exceed the marketability standards of more traditional resorts. These assumptions need to be thoroughly investigated through objective case studies.

3. Financial intermediary institutions need technical assistance and training in order to facilitate ecotourism project formulation, review and funding. Ecotourism workshops for participants from financial institutions in target countries could be an important step. These workshops would bring specialized interregional ecotourism teams to host countries to meet with representatives of local financial institutions and with local ecotourism entrepreneurs. Given that local banking institutions will be a vital link in the ecotourism finance chain, it is essential that they be given the information they need to act as informed intermediaries in the ecotourism development process.

4. A prefeasibility analysis fund should be established on a matching grant basis for ecotourism developments. This would allow ecotourism developers to bring proposals to the stage where they can be considered for key funding decisions. Given that prefeasibility analysis costs are in the hundreds of thousands of dollars, many developers never bring their proposals to the finance table due to the high up-front costs. Perhaps the fund could be similar to the Export Council for Renewable Energy (ECRE)'s prefeasibility study matching grants program, established by the renewable energy industry to assess the use of wind, gas and solar technology in developing countries.

5. International networking and information-sharing should be initiated. An interregional or international consortium might be formed to provide the following benefits:
   - Uniform standards;
   - quality control;
   - marketing coordination;
   - training and technical assistance;
   - access to capital;
   - information exchange;
   - education of local government officials.

These recommendations are made with the understanding that ecolodges are an important component of the ecotourism industry that need special technical assistance in gaining financing. Assistance of the kind proposed above will help local developers to build lodges that provide local conservation and sustainable development benefits. Globally, ecotourism has the potential to be a highly important economic development tool. More attention needs to be focused immediately on how to implement and finance ecotourism on the local level.

### Literature cited:

Summary of The Ecotourism Society Second Funding Policy Committee Meeting, Interamerican Investment Corporation, March 23, 1993. A formal summary of the meeting is available from.

Jorge Roldán. *Investing in Ecotourism Projects*, Document of the Interamerican Investment Corporation, June 1993, p. 7 and 10-14.

## Appendix:

### Multilateral Sources of Financing for Tourism Development

*Worldwide:*
International Bank for Reconstruction and
    Development – World Bank (IBRD)
International Finance Corporation (IFC)
The OPEC Fund for International Development
    (The OPEC Fund)

*Africa:*
African Development Bank (ADB)
East African Development Bank (EADB)
West African Development Bank (WADB)

*Americas:*
Interamerican Development Bank (IDB)
Central American Bank of Economic
    Integration (CABEI)
Caribbean Development Bank (CDB)

*Asia:*
Asian Development Bank (ADB)
Asian Development Fund (ADF)

*Europe:*
European Investment Bank (EIB)
European Development Fund (EDF)
European Bank for Reconstruction
    and Development (EBRD)

*Middle East:*
Islamic Development Bank (IDB)
Arab Fund for Economic and Social
    Development (AFESD)

*International Associations:*
Association of African Development Finance
    Institutions (AADFI)
Latin American Association of Development Finance
    Institutions (LAADFI)
Association of Development Financing Institutions in
    Asia and the Pacific (ADFIAP)

### Selected Development Banks, Multilateral and Bilateral Financing Sources

Overseas Private Investment Corporation
Canadian International Development Agency
European Investment Bank
German Finance Company for Investments in
    Developing Countries
Netherlands Development Finance Company
Industrialization Fund for Developing Countries
Overseas Economic Cooperation Fund of Japan
European Community Structural Funds
United Nations Development Program: Investment
    Feasibility Study Facility
Multilateral Investment Guarantee Agency

# Chapter 4:

# Resource Interpretation

# Ecotourism as Education

## Ecotourism as Education

The Chinese saying "Give a man a fish and he will eat for a day; teach him to fish and he will eat for a lifetime" rings true in its broader application to ecotourism as education. In this case, it might be phrased "Give people an ecotourism experience for a day and they will be impressed; teach them about ecotourism and it can change their lives."

If ecotourism is to promote responsible travel that conserves the natural environment and sustains the well-being of local people, then its foundation must rest on education. Such educational outreach should include both the local community and the international traveler. Lodge owners, like tour operators, can play a critical role in this process. Several examples of their creative approaches are described below.

## The Bush Classroom

Delta Camp, a small ecolodge facility in Botswana's Okavango Delta, was constructed primarily from local building materials and aimed at the high-end market of safari tourism. In an effort to support conservation education, promote an understanding of ecotourism among guests and provide high-quality training for its employees, Delta Camp came up with the idea of creating a bush school that would offer classes on wildlife ecology and conservation education. This "school" would be open to lodge staff, visiting students and local villagers working as guides.

Delta Camp proposed to build a thatch-roofed classroom under the trees and provide benches and a chalk board, if an outside educational institution would use the site to run field workshops on wildlife ecology, ecotourism and conservation. That was in 1992. The School for International Training, a U.S.-based college, and Tamu Safaris, a tour operator, agreed to participate in the project, and today the bush school initiated by Delta Camp hosts two workshops each year that bring together international visitors and local community guides to share information and learn about wildlife ecology and conservation in the Okavango Delta. It serves as an example of how one lodge owner with limited financial resources was able to create a successful ecotourism-as-education

*By Costas Christ*

program at his facility that benefits tourists, visiting students and local villagers alike.

It also shows how ecotourism as education can go beyond the simple interpretation of animal behaviors and ecology. When tourists learn about ecotourism by being participants themselves in the process – in this case an educational workshop for locals and visitors – they carry the experience with them when they travel in the future, choosing lodge facilities that adhere to an ecotourism philosophy. In that sense, ecotourism as education goes beyond a particular travel experience and begins to influence people's lives and how they travel – responsibly.

There are many ways in which lodge owners can become practitioners of ecotourism as education. These include creating information displays on the local environment, developing self-guided nature trails, having a naturalist or education director resident at the facility and providing pamphlets in guest rooms that explain local conservation efforts and the cultural values and traditions of the local people. These are all important steps in promoting responsible tourism and they send a clear educational message to the guests that originates with the lodge itself.

## The Lodge as Model

Another example of this type of ecotourism as education was created by the Conservation Corporation in Southern Africa (see page 104). After helping to establish the Phinda Resource Reserve in one of Southern Africa's richest areas of biodiversity, the Conservation Corporation designed and built the Phinda Forest Lodge – a luxury facility based on the principles of ecotourism. The lodge was constructed using many materials manufactured by local villagers. Trees were given the right of way. In several places, tree trunks replaced corner beams, and wooden decking was constructed around the growing trees. The entire lodge harmonizes with its environment: it stands on stilts, has windows instead of walls, and is small in size. It has become part of the tapestry of the forest itself. With guided nature walks, canoe trips and resident naturalists, the lodge embodies the ecotourism principles that the Conservation Corporation wishes to bring to every guest's attention. In this case,

the design and structure of a lodge, along with information and materials on the local culture and environment, supports ecotourism as education.

Teaching about ecotourism in principle and in practice, through a sustainable design, is as fundamental to a nature lodge or hotel as is good food or comfortable beds. People will remember the quality of their experience, especially if they feel they have learned something that has changed their lives. It is no wonder, then, that even large hotel chains such as Marriot and Intercontinental Hotels are developing portfolios at their properties that reflect the growing desire of travelers and tourists to stay in facilities that are friendly to the environment. It underscores how much influence ecotourism as education can have at the grass-roots level: A guest staying at a lodge who learns about conservation and ecology through education and interpretation will use this knowledge to select other ecotourism destinations and facilities. Education can also influence the tourist's attitude toward the finite natural resources of the planet. If they are North Americans, particularly, they begin to understand the implications of the fact that the United States of America, with less than one-sixth of the earth's population, continues to use nearly one-third of the world's natural resources.

## The Community Museum

Another example of ecotourism as education comes from the island of Lamu, Kenya. There, at the initiative of local community leaders, several lodge owners and tour operators contributed funding and support for the creation of a community marine environment museum. For the community, where generations have lived by the sea, the objective was to provide local people with a chance to learn more about the environment that continues to shape their lives. For lodge owners and tour operators, the incentive was to create a conservation education center that would also appeal to visiting tourists as an attraction and learning opportunity.

The key to effective ecotourism as education is to use every opportunity to enhance a visitor's experience through interpretation and education. This, of course, starts with the lodge design itself, which should incorporate interpretive exhibits that demonstrate resource protection concerns. But it should not be limited to exhibits and displays alone. The bush school and community environment museum described above show how lodge owners, tour operators and local communities can work together to promote education for mutual benefit.

## The Keepers of Culture

Nor is ecotourism as education concerned only with the natural environment. One of the most important aspects of interpretation and education at a lodge facility are guidelines and codes of ethics for visitors about local culture as well as ecology. An ecotourism facility should demonstrate the same sensitivity to local culture as it does to the natural environment; design should reflect the cultural resources of a region or country by incorporating cultural motifs and traditional styles wherever possible. Allowing visitors to see respect for local cultures in architectural design is in itself a form of education.

Again, an example from Lamu Island, Kenya. Approaching the Peponi Hotel in the ancient stone village of Shela, it is not clear where the hotel begins and the village ends. The facility was specifically designed to become a part of the village and to enhance, not detract from, the traditional Swahili architecture of the old stone houses. In this case, the hotel supports traditional cultural values by reinforcing and respecting them. The hotel itself becomes part of the educational process through which guests may learn about local culture.

At the Amandari Resort in Ubud, Bali, one of the most expensive facilities in Indonesia, the hotel supports the work of traditional dance instructors by operating a part-time dance school on the premises, where guests can also see performances. Fresh water can be scarce here, so the hotel was built to maintain the natural irrigation system of the rice terraces of local villagers. In so doing, the hotel encourages the preservation of traditional culture while also encouraging guests to learn about, appreciate and respect the local people and their values. This, too, is a form of ecotourism as education.

Like tour operators, lodge owners should be effective educators in preparing visitors for interacting with the natural and human environments they are visiting. And this means involving local people in the preparation process whenever possible. Finding out what is and is not acceptable behavior from tourists towards local people and making that information easily available to visitors teaches cultural sensitivity and results in better cross-cultural understanding.

## Conclusion: A Step-by-Step Process

Not long ago, I was asked by the director of tourism development in the Seychelles, "How can we call ourselves an ecotourism destination when so many of our hotels and lodges were built at a time when awareness of environmentally or culturally sensitive resort design was lacking?" This is a question that continues to come up in many countries interested in developing a national ecotourism plan. Lodge and hotel owners representing properties built when ecotourism wasn't even a topic for discussion are intimidated by all they hear they should do to meet standards of ecotourism. The point is not to be intimidated, but to realize that whether a lodge is old or new, there are many ways, step by step, to build opportunities for ecotourism as education into a visitor's experience. All of the examples mentioned here are lodge or hotel facilities designed and built well before ecotourism became popular. And yet, through creative initiative and commitment to the ideals of educating tourists to be environmentally and culturally sensitive, these properties are now some of the finer models of ecotourism today.

The key to success is in the commitment to the process. By definition, ecotourism is education – a way for tourists to learn how to have a more positive impact on the natural and human environment in the areas they visit. Lodge owners, like tour operators, are in a unique position to act as facilitators and teachers within the tourism industry for that learning to take place.

# Educational Approaches and Interpretive Trends in Ecotourism

*By Craig R. Sholley*

## Ecotourist Expectations

Natural history and cultural interpretation have always been an important ingredient in the ecotourism thought process. As the concept and philosophy of ecotourism continue to evolve, the educational component is becoming increasingly significant and has been elevated to a priority in most ecotours. Ecotourist educational expectations have steadily increased; today's sophisticated client demands high levels of natural history and cultural content and a variety of presentations and experiences. Evolving ecotourism standards and ecotourist demands have, therefore, been a major impetus behind increased emphasis on education among nature tour and lodge operators and trip program designers. This has prompted new and creative forms of training, presentation and individual field instruction. This paper will summarize the broad educational strategy devised by leaders in the ecotourism industry and offer examples of successful and imaginative approaches to nature interpretation.

## Educating the Educators

One of the single most important elements of a safe, memorable and educationally rewarding nature travel experience is the talents and skill level of the naturalist guide. Ecotourism principles dictate the careful selection, hiring and, if required, subsequent training of *resident local* experts. Ongoing in-house training and off-site coursework should become an integral feature of the naturalist's job requirements and ultimately enhance future programs and naturalist/trip participant interactions.

Costa Rica Expeditions, a Central American-based inbound operator, annually sponsors a staff retreat with presentations by regional and international experts, and with role-playing and problem-solving sessions to motivate, direct and better prepare naturalists to fulfill their educational and professional roles when leading tours. In contrast, International Expeditions, a U.S.-based nature tour company, has developed a workshop trip format for clients, with opportunities to interact with scientists and conservationists during hands-on field-oriented activities.

Emphasizing the importance of the ecological relationships in specific habitats (i.e., Peruvian rainforests and the East African savannahs), internationally renowned research and conservation experts present field sessions in their areas of expertise. International Expeditions and its in-country operators have strongly supported and encouraged participation in these workshops by all of their local guides. Participating in the workshops alongside workshop clients and treated similarly, the naturalist guides have enthusiastically responded. They have quickly incorporated new information into their formal and informal presentations, enhancing the educational content of their clients' trips.

An exciting offshoot of the Rainforest and Savannah Workshops has been Teacher Workshops for the professional educator and secondary education program development. Teacher Workshops have also provided participating U.S.-based teachers with the mechanism to organize Student Workshops for teenage groups. During Student Workshops, teachers collaborate with naturalist guides with whom they've already shared a workshop, and offer their students a similar experience. The result is a continually expanding educational adventure.

## Opportunities for Discovery

Spontaneous on-site interpretation is key to the success of an ecotour. The role of the naturalist guide is well substantiated in this regard. However, interpretive activities cannot be confined only to naturalist and trip participant interactions. Many ecotourists join a tour or arrive at a lodge facility with limited natural history/cultural expertise; others are more informed. In either case, they anticipate some guidance, but also expect opportunities to explore and discover using their existing knowledge.

To support these individualized activities, ecolodges must make the region around their facilities safely and easily accessible for lodge visitors. Well-marked trails and self-guided trail brochures strengthen individualized exploration. The trails and support brochures often provide only general information on regional habitat and its inhabitants. More recently, developed trails are theme-based and orient

hikers to a specific concept or series of connected ideas. An example of the theme-based trail is the Medicinal Plant Trail which runs around the periphery of the Amazon Center for Environmental Education and Research (ACEER) in Peru. Supporting an integrated combination of tourism, education and research, the trail was designed by visiting ethnobotanists and local shamans and now serves a range of purposes from pure science to local student education and sound ecotourism. Plants are identified by number and referenced in a brochure available at the lodge. Their medicinal uses are simply described in the brochure, but may be further explored in a reference guide at the lodge. The guide was recently published by scientists working in conjunction with the ACEER. Similarly, the entire region around the ACEER has been biologically surveyed, providing scientists and ecotourists with complete mammal, bird and floral lists. These printed lists are also available at the ACEER lodge and help tourists make the most of their discovery adventures.

Scientific research and field conservation which provide important links to the expanding educational and informational base of ecotour programming have also led to creative ecotour activities. Again, the ACEER and its affiliate International Expeditions provide an exciting example. Prompted by discussions with leading Amazon rainforest canopy scientists and ACEER board members, International Expeditions conceived and constructed a Canopy Walkway. This extensive multi-level system of aerial platforms and pathways is designed to be ecologically sensitive to the living rainforest. The walkway enables scientists, tourists, local inhabitants and educators to study, observe and experience the most dynamic dimension of the rainforest, previously inaccessible.

Study groups from Missouri Botanical Gardens, Samford University, Pittsburgh State University, University of Michigan and the National Museum of Natural History are just some of the institutions benefiting from this novel approach to rainforest exploration and education. In turn, they have added to our knowledge of this complex ecosystem. Integrated scientific research and ecotour education have thus indirectly led to the exploration of renewable rainforest resources and discovery of potential benefits to the local population. These discoveries are leading to important justifications for further protection of the prolific, but fragile, rainforest biome.

## Conclusion: An Evolving Process

Ecotourism philosophy and practices continue to evolve rapidly. Nature interpretation and conservation education increasingly will become important factors guiding the process. Their professional, creative and ethical incorporation into the ecotourism process will allow us to study, appreciate and preserve our earth's ecosystems.

# Interpretation Guidelines

## "The Art of Guiding"

*By Oswaldo Muñoz*

## Introduction

It is often thought that field interpretation techniques are solely within the domain of a biologist, and that guiding is a less important role in tourism operations. This unfortunate situation arises from the false conviction that ecotourism is synonymous with nature tourism, and thus the liaison between the ecotourist and the eco-site is necessarily better in the hands of a natural science major than a tour guide. In my travels, I have at times even encountered antagonistic and/or competitive attitudes between so-called tour guides and resident scientists at biological field stations, as a result of their not having defined their respective roles and, most importantly, not having perfected and coordinated their efforts when dealing with visitors. Guiding should encompass not only the ability to explain to the traveler the area being visited, or to coordinate with the tourism operator, but to convey the all-important message that true ecotourism entails: The importance of sustainable lifestyles, both at home and abroad. It is for these reasons that a new breed of professional tour guide, duly trained in the art of motivation through effective communication, is increasingly in demand.

The following paper is based on practical experiences and observations I have examined and studied in the field of guiding throughout the past 27 years. I have addressed these ideas not only to tourism guides and biologists, but to local ground ecotourism operators who must be aware of what is expected of their "field representatives" along with the support and coordination that should be provided by their operations department.

## Basic Guiding Techniques

### Guidelines for Guests

The first impression on any tour is the lasting impression. Many tour groups are met at the airport by a guide at the beginning of their trip itinerary, or later when the group is off to its first visitor site. These are crucial moments when the guide can either get things off to a good start or drag a series of problems throughout the tour. Consequently, by following these simple recommendations, a number of potential problems and misinterpretations could be avoided, making life easier for both guide and tourist, right from the start. Above all, consider that, no matter how obvious something may appear in the eyes of the guide, he or she should never overestimate a guest's perspective or intuitive abilities when in another country.

1. *Expectations.* Encourage an acceptance of a country and/or site for what it is and not for what would initially be expected of it. This will eliminate unreasonable demands and strains placed on eco-sites or logistical arrangements.

2. *Adaptation.* Stimulate visitors into adjusting to the different ecosystems and environments (climate, food, accommodations) as a highlight of their travel experience.

3. *The country's system.* Encourage and advise guests on the ways things get done or never get done in the host country, viewing this cultural experience as an asset to the uniqueness of the trip.

4. *Day-by-day.* Suggest visitors take it one day at a time to avoid unnecessary worry over future events in the program, thus contributing to the participants' ease and enjoyment.

5. *Teamwork.* Encourage active participation so that successful outcomes can be the product of everyone's input, giving visitors a sense of accomplishment.

6. *Guide/visitor relationship.* Convert this initial, lineal association into a reciprocal "friend/guest" connection, where both parties will benefit from each other's information and knowledge.

7. *Interaction.* Assist guests in communicating with the people of a country as a means of enriching their experience, while overseeing this contact to avoid cultural errors.

8. *Photography.* Advise visitors about the importance of cultural reactions to being photographed, suggesting that "objectification" be replaced by humanistic interest. Explain to your guests what they are photographing, especially concerning natives, whenever such photo opportunities are feasible.

9. *Communication.* Ask guests to communicate to you or the pertinent staff member if they have any problem or complaint the moment an issue presents itself.

10. *Rules and regulations.* The observance of these are meant to enhance the safety and well-being of guests, sites visited and general operation.

11. *Sense of values.* Discourage guests from making direct comparisons between countries, as economic, social and political factors are intimately related to cultural and ethnic characteristics. Treated independently of other societies, a country can be better understood.

12. *Enthusiasm.* Make it understood that enthusiasm is reciprocal; it is instrumental in starting the guide's "information generator." The more they ask, the more they will learn and enjoy.

## Guidelines for Guides

1. *Be well informed of the most current local and global news, including environmental issues.* First thing in the morning, read the newspaper. Ask guests first if they wish to hear the news or not; quite a few like to take a vacation away from all news media on an ecotour, but that is not an excuse for a guide not knowing current happenings.

2. *Abide by a "code of ethics" for guides.* If non-existent, in the interim incorporate your own environmental and professional sensitivity in carrying out your activity.

3. *Take along your portable "guide kit,"* including field notebook, trail maps, charts, reference books, checklists, binoculars, first aid, etc.

4. *Have guests observe the official rules and regulations for visitor sites.* If none exist, seek to incorporate your own environmental concern in the establishment of preliminary visiting guidelines, while requesting professional and official assistance to have the rules drawn up.

5. *Motivate tourists on the importance of environmental issues,* regionally and globally, so that their visit to an eco-site becomes a stepping stone towards the cause of conservation and rational use of resources, both at home and abroad.

6. *Help monitor environmental impacts,* including tourism-related activities, in coordination with government authorities. As Francisco Dallmeier of the Smithsonian "Man and the Biosphere" program proposes, "With adequate training, operators and guides could take on decisive roles as 'biodiversity physicians' when helping to monitor protected areas."

7. *Improve your guiding techniques and general knowledge.* Attend seminars and workshops regularly. Through guiding associations or clubs, guides could share their particular expertise or skills. For example, each month a guide could give a formal presentation on some subject to the rest of his/her associates.

8. *Plan your talks and lectures* in coordination with the group leader or local expert.

9. *Intercede when necessary in the interaction between guests and the site* being visited in order to minimize any major impact.

10. *Learn to say "I don't know"* if an answer to a question is not possible. It is not an obligation to "know everything." More importantly, it is not only how much you know but how well you can convey that information to your guests.

11. *Keep your promises to your guests,* and never offer something that is not truly or totally feasible, such as a clear day or thirty life birds on one field trip.

12. *Fine-tune your perception of difficulty, time and space.* This means to be as accurate and realistic as possible when announcing traveling time or distances between regions and sites or actual lengths of walks. Likewise, be accurate as to the degree of difficulty on certain treks or river trips. It is safer to magnify the distance to a place or the difficulty in a walk than to underestimate it.

13. *Discourage giving plastic or non-biodegradable gifts to local communities,* especially in the more remote regions, while stimulating "cultural" rather than "commodity" exchange between visitors and natives.

14. *Use common sense and be honest.*

## More Hints and Ideas

The skills involved in professional guiding are honed as a result of a constant learning process. Your own initiative and imagination are essential in developing personalized techniques. With this in mind, consider adapting the following suggestions to your own needs and interests.

1. *About guest books.* From experience, I have found that guest books at lodges could be a problem in raising people's expectations. When a guest reads about a previous group seeing a particularly rare species, the guide might find himself with the challenge of having to equal or surpass that experience. Thus, I would recommend handing out "guest sheets" to be inserted into a loose-leaf book to be hard bound year by year for the hotel's personal and confidential record.

2. *About using slides and videos for briefings.* In many lodges, slides and/or videos are used to explain what will be seen and done the following day. This contributes to anticlimactic or even disappointing experiences at a visitor site when an activity does not live up to what was visually offered the day before. The excitement of unexpected surprises is thus eclipsed. It is better to select slides of what was actually seen or experienced earlier that day as a means of reviewing or elaborating on certain themes, rather than anticipating possibilities, especially regarding wildlife.

3. *Learn to interpret holistically.* Quite often, there are many more features to interpret at an ecosite than the most obvious ones. For example, viewing the ancient ruins at Palenque there is archaeology, obviously; geology – the type of stones used to build the temples; climatology – what is the weather pattern at the site and why? ethnobotany – how does the present-day community use botanical species in their herbal medicine? ornithology – the species name of that bird perched on top of the ruins; linguistics – what language do the past and present cultures speak in the region? geobotany – what are some of the introduced plant species and crops found on the way to the site and their place of origin? Thus, being a guide in natural surroundings does not

necessarily imply that you are solely a naturalist. Guiding is far more interesting for the guide and the visitors when a great realm of topics can be treated at a site.

4. *Today's reading.* There are great excerpt and quotations from books that can be read to the guests after dinner. Guides can gather their own material, making sure that the same is highly interesting and stimulating.

5. *Lectures that promote conservation.* The Ecotourism Society defines ecotourism as "responsible travel that conserves the environment and sustains the well-being of local peoples." Thus, as naturalist guides, it is your duty to educate your guests in the principles of conservation some time during the trip. Gather material and excerpts from books and papers on conservation and environmentalism that could be used as material during such lectures, in order to have tourists not only "visit nature with reverence" but "come home changed."

## Know Your "Product" – What Makes it Tick

Just like the salesperson, in guiding you must be familiar with the eco-site in order to do your job skillfully and professionally. To exemplify this concept, I would like to present the following analogy between selling a vacuum cleaner and interpreting an element at an ecosite, such as a kapok tree.

THE PRODUCT:

| A VACUUM CLEANER | A KAPOK TREE |
| --- | --- |
| How does it work? | How does it grow? |
| Technical description | Biological features |
| Raw materials needed for production | Ecological relationships |
| Manufacturing process | Plant physiology |
| Quality control | Environmental conservation |
| Characteristics | Practical uses of the tree |
| Warranty | Rational use of natural resources |

## Captivating the Tourists – Selling Them on an Eco-destination

The guide must capture the clients' attention in order to nurture their interest, which will be reinforced in the field, stimulating motivation to take action.

ATTENTION → INTEREST → REINFORCEMENT → MOTIVATION → ACTION

The interest is thus transformed into the conviction about the importance of the total message that is backing the guide's performance – and the image of the company and the country he/she represents. The conviction will thus motivate the client to take action in several ways:

- Becoming a more conscientious individual regarding the rational use of natural and human resources, both at home and abroad;

- joining an environmental/conservation organization back home;

- donating money for a conservation project in the host country or, more specifically, to support the site visited;

- promoting the professionalism and commitment of the inbound as well as outbound operator (word-of-mouth publicity accounts for 70% of all successful promotional campaigns about a tourist destination);

- possible economic reward (tip) to the guide, crew and/or local community participants for a job well done.

Remember: The first impression in the eyes of the tourist is vital, since a second chance might never come.

## Conclusion

Once the general guidelines have been identified, there is a constant need for innovation as one guides over the years – something that goes beyond inventiveness. Change and motivation in the guest and guide are the most important end results that must be achieved through professional guiding. Once those goals are met, all other priorities are addressed.

# Interpretation of Tropical Rainforests for Ecotourists

*By Gerardo Budowski*

## Introduction

The spectacular growth of ecotourism, much faster than the tourism industry in general, has been eloquently demonstrated. Among the various ecotourism attractions in tropical countries, possibly the most significant increase has been related to the "exploitation" of the forests, particularly the many types of tropical rainforests. True, such appreciation of the rainforests is a recent phenomenon, prevalent in a few countries and often only in a few areas, but it is clearly a trend as has been shown in developments taking place in Costa Rica, Ecuador, Brazil, Amazonian Peru, Bolivia, Belize and Panama, where the forest has become a lucrative tourist destination.

The present analysis aims to review our knowledge with particular attention to interpretation of the many features encountered in the rain forests, but problems will also be brought into focus. They are based on experience from four decades as a tropical forester, some previous publications on the subject (Budowski, 1973, 1976, 1991, 1993, 1994) and as the designer of three trails for walking into the forest, all of them in Costa Rica but within ecologically different locations.

## The Tropical Deforestation Crisis: Why Can Ecotourism Help?

Deforestation in tropical forested countries has been and still is an extremely critical aspect of land use which has triggered a worldwide interest in stopping and reverting the process, but so far with limited success. Certainly it is not easy when powerful economic and social forces tend to favor conversion of the forests to other uses.

In the last 20 years, great efforts have been undertaken by conservationists and others bent on preserving the forests through careful exploitation schemes where sustainability is the main factor. Sustainable management for timber is an example. At this moment worldwide, only about 1% of all natural forests that are being exploited can be labeled to be so "on a sustainable basis." In fact, in much of tropical Latin American countries where logging of tropical forests is prevalent, over 80% of all forests logged in the last 20 years do not exist anymore.

Management for nontimber products and services is much less destructive than logging. Great efforts are presently being made to enhance the value of all these products to make it obvious that management benefits local populations and can be economically rewarding and socially acceptable. There are also services derived from the presence of forests. Some are difficult to quantify. Rainforests, for example, cover only 0.64% of land surface, but hold 30-40% of all living land species. Finally there is ecotourism, another tool to enhance the value of the forests. Judging from the ever increasing number of national parks and other categories of protected areas, there is obviously a relationship between the interests of tourism in rainforests and those planning and managing protected areas. While the promotion of ecotourism is generally not the prime motive for creating these protected forest areas, it has in fact stimulated forest protection because it provides income on a national and local scale. Some large protected areas are "zoned," allowing for visitation in some parts while others are strictly protected.

But ecotourism can also cause damage when not properly managed. It is therefore important that ecotourism in forest areas be properly planned and controlled. This implies overcoming a series of hurdles that need to be carefully analyzed if ecotourism is to be a continuously successful tool for conservation.

## Overcoming Negative Attitudes of Visitors to Tropical Forests

For many people, particularly those not acquainted with tropical forests, there is a sense of danger when entering the rainforest, from snakes, stinging insects, leeches, attacking fishes or other dangerous animals – or even people – as has unfortunately been publicized or hinted in legends, adventure publications or movies. Most of it makes no sense; the feared piranhas or army ants or snakes are good cases of what constitute very low-risk phenomena. Moreover, many species that may pose some danger can be easily avoided by better knowledge of animal habits.

Then there is a feeling of helplessness when one is confronted with the immense diversity of the tropical rainforest by the sheer number of species, particularly plants and insects. Our knowledge is quickly improving not only concerning the number of species but also the multitude of interactions between plants, animals and their physical environment.

Visitors who explore tropical rainforests should be given instructions as to how they should behave. Different codes of ethics are available.

## Interpretation: The Key to Attracting Satisfied Ecotourists

The great diversity of life forms and natural settings in the rainforest allow for a great variety of interpretative features. This includes water courses, swamps, rocks and all their inherent characteristics.

Good interpretation is based on knowledge in different fields such as ecology, botany, zoology and their various interactions, presented as an exciting experience for the visitor. Almost 20 years ago in a meeting on ecological guidelines for humid tropical lands, a notable tropical forester, Frank Wadsworth, saw the potential when he wrote,"The tropical American forests with their giant trees, spectacular animal life and the background of mountains and rivers, should be considered as a nondeveloped scenic resource, with a tremendous economic potential, to be exported to the whole world, possibly to be compared with the wildlife spectacle of Central East Africa" (Wadsworth, 1976).

Interpretation very much depends on the quality of tourist guides, the various publications and the briefing given to ecotourists before entering the forests. In some countries, special efforts are being made to train local guides living close to the ecotourist resource being visited.

## Some Experiences in Designing Nature Trails in Tropical Rainforests

1.  The trail should not be longer than 1.5 kilometers, on relatively flat grounds. Longer trails may be designed for adventurous people, but the average for the general public may be best around 800-1200 meters.

2. It should preferably be circular or oval in shape, so that head-on traffic is avoided.

3. It is important to look for variety to provide the maximum of experiences to the visitor. It is generally easy, for example, to have the trail pass through both primary and secondary forests, or close to very large trees with spectacular buttresses of different shapes, or large woody lianas; it is desirable to alternate relatively open areas with others of dense shade; the crossing of a creek close to a small waterfall or a small swamp is always desirable if appropriate rustic bridges or elevated walkways can be built.

4. When there is a large number of visitors, it is not advisable to walk on the soil since this creates compaction and some sinking, followed by puddles, since quick water infiltration is impeded by compaction. On steep terrain, erosion can be serious. There are many ways of solving the problems depending on costs and numbers of visitors. The ideal is elevated trails since they interfere least with natural processes. But they are costly and need careful maintenance in these wet environments. In some places, cemented trails have been built. They have obvious advantages and drawbacks. They allow visitors to look up or further along the trails, instead of carefully watching their steps. Another very common solution is to place slabs of nonperishable lumber covered with dense chicken wire that has been nailed on the downward face. The wire prevents falling on slippery surfaces. In some trails, a cover of coarse sand has been useful. On steep slopes, steps covered with wood slabs with chicken wire are often used. Drainage ditches must of course be considered here as well.

5. It is desirable to avoid signs or inscriptions except those indispensable for orientation or warning. Although the use of botanical identifications or well protected inscriptions on different stops is often practiced, it appears preferable to use only numbers for the stops within the forests with a small publication giving an explanation for each stop. The printed material can be illustrated with drawings of the features displayed and a map of the trail but may have to be revised from time to time. An outstanding example of this type of publication is the excellent guide by Wong and Ventocilla (1986) for Barro Colorado in Panama.

6. It is desirable to brief tourists before entering the trail. This is best done at a small visitor center (or large, according to budget and number of visitors). Not only should visitors be instructed about possible (and imaginary) dangers, but they should also be encouraged to read some materials and look at trail maps and various relevant posters. Specific queries and possible fears should be dispelled. A toilet should be installed here.

7. The spacing of different groups of visitors into the forest should become a general rule, since what visitors usually want to see least are other groups of ecotourists along the trails. If a guide is required to join the visitors, he or she should not cover more than twelve persons since it is much more difficult to address larger groups along the trail. A loudspeaker is not desirable because of its disruptive effect. Visitors should always stay along trails unless allowed otherwise.

8. It cannot be repeated too often that the guides are the key element to make a visit through the forest an enjoyable experience. They should not only be competent in the biological field but also understand psychological traits of the visitors. They must carefully identify their audiences, their specific interests and strengths as well as their limitations (physical, cultural or other). In some countries, special efforts are being made to train local guides living close to the ecotourist resource. If it is a self-guided tour, high-quality printed materials are of course indispensable.

9. Rain can be a disturbing factor and must be dealt with according to audiences. Some people simply don't mind as long as they keep moving. Others need raincoats or small umbrellas.

## Common Features to Interpret

There are thousands of worthwhile features that can be shown and interpreted to visitors, depending on sites. The following is a list of sights applicable to the

American tropics based mostly on plant life or commonly found animals, usually very popular with most tourists. The picture is different with special groups such as ornithologists or those coming specifically to see certain plants, mammals or reptiles.

1.  Ant nests and ant trails with workers carrying leaves or other plant pieces (sometimes even other insects, according to species). Termite nests and their protected trails along the branches (with a good explanation about their role in helping to decompose dead branches) are usually easily found.

2.  Large buttresses of trees are always spectacular and a popular feature. There are many types of buttresses and much has been written about their function and patterns of growth. It may be worth to point out that some very large trees (e.g., *Anacardium excelsum*) have no buttresses at all, although in forests with high annual rainfall, superficial roots are the rule and they often appear at great distances from the stem.

3.  Strangler figs (and clusias) are usually found; their origin and development are fascinating.

4.  Large woody lianas and their role in the community will also elicit interesting interpretations. Some may attain over 100 meters in length and display considerable growth pattern variations whether in the shade or in the crowns.

5.  Epiphytes with their amazing display of families, species life forms and their role in the community are always popular. There are sometimes over fifty different species growing on a single tree among aroids, orchids, ferns, mosses, cacti, lichens and so on. Particularly spectacular are the various bromeliads with water tanks where many insects, frogs, salamanders and small snakes may be found.

6.  Palms in all their variety allow for interesting observations. At first sight, at least, in Costa Rica, many of the small undergrowth palms look very much the same, but careful perusal reveals differences in leaf forms, fruiting patterns and growth forms. Some are not even botanically classified under palms (*Cyclanthaceae*).

7.  There is usually a large variety of animals on display although they may be small. Besides ants and termites, birds are a great attraction. Frogs, iguanas and other lizards are commonly seen, while crocodiles may be found along rivers or swamps. Guides should learn about the season when certain trees bear flowers or fruits that attract certain birds, monkeys or bats. The ground under certain fruiting trees (including palms) allows for interesting observations of animal presence.

8.  Fallen trees create gaps and trigger successional processes allowing interpretation of the gradual replacement with incoming secondary species.

9.  Night trips – carefully organized – can add to the attraction since many new nocturnal creatures can be found. Experienced guides, though, may be required.

## Follow-up Education and Improvement of Trail

1.  Secondary trails branching out from the main trail may be planned to provide visitors with an appreciation of additional forest features.

2.  Scientists from different disciplines should be tapped for additional interpretation along the trail. The guides, and even ecotourists on a self-guided trip, should also be encouraged to report new data.

3.  Surveys may be designed for different audiences to help determine visitors' perceptions and prepare improvements.

4.  New trails to relieve pressure on excessively popular trails may be planned.

5.  In some exceptional areas, innovations may include designing trails for the blind along a wire with braille inscriptions as well as for the physically handicapped (on relatively flat, cemented trails). Some examples already exist.

In summary, the design of nature trails in tropical rainforests can be a powerful tool to enhance the value of these forests and allow for their conservation. It is a relatively new interpretation tool creating worthwhile experiences and education.

## Literature cited:

Budowski, Gerardo. 1973. *Tourism and Environmental Conservation: Conflict, Coexistence or Conflict?* Keynote address PATA Conference. Kyoto. Reproduced in Environmental Conservation 3(1) 27-31. 1976 and Parks 1(4) 3-6. 1977.

_____. 1991. *Los Bosques Tropicales y el Ecoturismo.* In Johnson Dennis, ed. Proceeding of the Humid Tropical Lowlands Conference. vol. IV, pp. 25-35.

_____. 1993. *Ecoturismo en los Parques Nacionales de Costa Rica.* In I Seminario Venezolano de Ecoturismo 4-5 de Octubre 1993. Caracas, Venezuela. 7p. Mimeografiado.

_____. 1994. *Turismo Sustentable con Enfasis en Ecoturismo: las Nuevas Tendencias en el Mercado Mundial.* Inaugural Lecture of the Turismo sustentable (ecoturismo), COTAL 94. XXXVII Congress, Madrid, May 29-June 3, 1994. In press.

Wadsworth, F.N. 1976. *Los Bosques Naturales en el Desarrollo de las Regiones Tropicales Humedas Americanas.* In Poore, Duncan, ed. *The Natural Forests in the Development of Humid American Tropics.* Internal Union for the Conservation of Nature, Switzerland. 361 pp. 185-198.

Wong, Marina and Ventocilla, Jorge. 1986. *A Day on Barro Colorado Island.* Panama Smithsonian Tropical Research Institute. 93 pp.

# EL PORTAL TROPICAL FOREST CENTER

*Commonwealth of Puerto Rico*

El Portal Tropical Forest Center is located in the Caribbean National Forest in the Commonwealth of Puerto Rico. The forest, known locally as El Yunque, is part of the Sierra Luquillo Mountains southeast of San Juan. Designed by Edward D. Stone & Associates, the project is being constructed under the supervision of the U.S. Forest Service which also has the responsibility to manage this unique resource.

In an attempt to identify current users, the U.S. Forest Service initiated a multi-year research program in 1989. The study identified thirteen groups, of which four were dominant:

| Percentage of Total Visitors | Type of Visitor | Length of Stay |
|---|---|---|
| 29% | Urban Visitors | 2.5 Hours |
| 55% | International Visitors | 1 Hour |
| 2% | Nature Tourist | 2-3 Days |
| 14% | Rural Visitors | 5 Hours |

*(Estimated 1988 figures; 635,100 visitors)*

Students are becoming a more important user group with great potential for growth. The number of student visitors to El Yunque is expected to increase from 14,000 to 30,000 in the coming years.

The needs of these diverse user groups were considered in the formation of the program for El Portal. Factors such as language, recreational purpose, knowledge levels of ecosystems and length of stay influenced the physical planning and interpretive messages.

El Portal is designed to fulfill two major roles identified in the study:

## Visitor Center

El Portal will be an interpretive center welcoming thousands of visitors annually and providing them an opportunity to learn about and enjoy the natural beauty of the rainforest. Vital information about the forest, Puerto Rican culture and global issues affecting all rainforests will be disseminated and interpreted.

## Training Facility

El Portal will provide a base station for researchers to study worldwide issues like deforestation and the complex subject of forest management. El Portal's conference center will provide space for both seminars and short-term research projects. The complex will be connected to a worldwide network through its satellite link, allowing researchers to participate in teleconferences and educational events throughout the world and to exchange database information with other centers.

Two-bedroom casitas, dispersed along a "street setting" reminiscent of rural Puerto Rican towns, will provide housing and work space for visiting researchers and students. La Casa Grande, with a covered dining terrace that offers ocean views, will provide both dining and social space for residents.

Finally, a self-guided tour with audio tapes will lead visitors through a nursery demonstration area of tropical woods and showcase sustainable timber products. The nursery will also grow native trees for use in reforestation projects and for sale to the public.

– Michael Champagne
Edward D. Stone & Associates

*Chapter 5:*

# Ecolodge Guidelines and Standards

# How Green Is My Ecolodge: Eco-Labeling Evaluation Issues and Criteria

*By Peter Williams, Ph.D.*

## Introduction

An unprecedented greening of business in the western world is underway, with a wide range of products and services touted to be environmentally friendly flooding the market. This trend is in response to a marketplace that has become more environmentally aware and committed to practicing greener forms of behavior than ever before. What was expressed as an intellectual commitment to the environment in the past is now being translated into specific forms of on-the-ground action. Numerous opinion surveys attest to the priority consumers give environmental issues. Findings emanating from a broad spectrum of consumer studies attest to the high priority being placed on government, corporate and individual actions which support environmental initiatives (Williams, 1993). Where past images and attitudes set "environmentalists" squarely in a negative light, more recent trends position them closer to the mainstream of society. Environmentalists are just as likely to be working within manufacturing or retail organizations as they are to be found toiling for special interest advocacy groups.

This greening of the marketplace should not be taken as some sort of fad or fashion. There is a growing outcry against irresponsible environmental behavior, and more and more the marketplace is advocating environmental sensitivity in all aspects of our interaction with the earth and its resources. According to the Travel Industry Association of America, in the United States alone there are over 43 million people who consider themselves to be self-proclaimed "ecotourists" who are willing to pay more for environmentally friendly travel products. Green consumerism is viewed by many people as an important route towards achieving a more environmentally friendly world. The response to shift in attitudes and behaviors is being expressed in a variety of ways.

## Eco-Speak

A whole new jargon has emerged to express the subtleties and nuances that differentiate the environmentally focused world from its industrially driven counterpart. This spectrum of language ranges from commercially focused eco-sell jargon associated with the marketing of green products and services to more values-oriented phrases in politically correct forms of expression. These expressions reflect the shifting of perspectives on what constitutes environmentally responsible behavior.

For example, it is unlikely that a decade ago terms such as PCBs, UVs, CFCs, toxicity accumulation, biodegradability, waste stream reduction technologies, composting agents, agro-diversity, ambient noise thresholds, ozone depletion, packaging protocols and "cradle-to-grave" environmental management were used in common conversation. Today such expressions are mainstream for most university students and are becoming part of the vocabulary for a good portion of the general public. Similarly, a decade ago the tourism industry had only begun to conceive such terms as responsible, appropriate, alternative, low-impact, eco- or green tourism (Valentine 1992). Today the buzzwords of the industry include expressions like cumulative impact, cultural sensitivity, eco-codes, environmental auditing and green management systems. In all of these cases it is unlikely that people always understand the specific meaning of these expressions. However, they do signal a strong and growing personal and corporate predisposition and awareness about the importance of protecting the resources on which the industry depends (Lenhart, 1994).

## Eco-Marketing

From a business perspective, it makes sense to use the fact that green sells to develop innovative product lines and services which meet the psychological and basic needs of today's environmentally conscious consumers. Ethically correct or otherwise, consumers can be made to feel good about their decision to protect the environment by purchasing eco-products. The real issue is whether or not they end up being lulled into complacency, feeling that little else needs to be done. People have a tendency to become placated by their "feel-good" green shopping habits, and forget larger issues. Whether buying a box of detergent or purchasing an exotic travel holiday, people require the information necessary to make the choice (Clabon, 1994). While it is the consumer who eventually will make the purchase decision, good marketing practice

entails providing as much of the required intelligence information as possible needed to direct the consumer toward the desired result (Carson and Moulden, 1991).

More and more the information requirements relate to specific environmental concerns. Automobile manufacturers extol the emission standards of their cars, agricultural producers promote the organic features of their produce, builders profile the energy efficiencies of their building designs, and beverage suppliers highlight their chemical-free drinks. The same is occurring in tourism operations. Airlines promote the reduced noise levels of their aircraft, hotels underscore the "energy-smart" technologies of their operations, restaurants detail the strengths of their food waste reduction programs, mass tour operators proclaim the energy efficiencies of their cruise and bus carriers and adventure destinations advertise their commitments to low-impact touring practices (WTTC, 1993).

Much of this is done in the name of maintaining and improving market share with a segment of the population that is growing in size and importance. The market-driven nature of tourism plays a significant role in determining what changes are taking place. Much of this change comes not from a deep-seated conviction on the part of tourism companies to tour gently on the globe, but rather from a growing pressure among traveling consumers to do what is responsible and meaningful for the earth's environment (Masterton, 1994).

## Eco-Labeling

The marketing strategies of many corporations have led not only to the publication of product information about the environmental characteristics of specific types of products, but also to the growth of eco-labels. Developed by product producing companies, government organizations and independent non-governmental organizations, these eco-labeling initiatives have been designed to help consumers make informed decisions on the purchase and use of specific products and services (Environment Canada, 1993). For example, environmental labeling programs have been developed for everything from packaging to manufacturing processes. In tourism, we have witnessed the development of eco-labeling programs by a wide variety of organizations for a range of reasons. These include PATA's Green Leaf, WTTC's Green Globe, Germany's Green Suitcase, Denmark's upcoming Green Key and Europe's Blue Flag programs. In most cases, their publicly stated reason for existence has been to encourage tourism organizations and businesses to become more environmentally friendly in their operations (Hawkes and Williams, 1993). Less altruistic reasons for their presence include opportunities to gain a competitive advantage over other businesses by:

- Using the eco-label in their market positioning strategies through corporate advertising and branding;

- gaining public recognition as an ethical and environmentally responsible business through extensive public relations activities associated with the eco-label;

- networking with a variety of environmentally focused industry practitioners and specialists familiar with the most cost-effective and efficient ways of implementing environmental practices;

- enhancing their image as good environmental citizens and employers through affiliation with the eco-label.

In a broader context, in many instances the proliferation of these labels has resulted in consumer confusion, to the devaluation of all of the labels and the particular detriment of those labels for which award criteria are particularly stringent (Strid and Carter, 1992). For products in many sectors of the economy, it is becoming increasingly difficult to establish and remember which labels are awarded on the basis of objective assessment processes and which are merely eye-catching logos. Is a label any more significant if it is based on the extent to which it adheres to one specific set of criteria or another? Is the problem limited to distinguishing between real labels and cosmetic ones? For instance, it is often difficult for a consumer to establish the merits of environmentally friendly claims – does it really matter if a product is more one thing than another? From an environmental perspective there may be arguments both ways. Even motivated consumers who explore these positions will often find themselves faced with a choice between information provided by a pressure group on the one hand and claims by product representatives on the other. In such a context, it may be difficult to judge whether either side is presenting anything other than propaganda, or even if there is some middle ground in between. All of this information creates a "noise" in the consumer's mind that is breeding a growing cynicism about environmental claims and labels. The outcome of it all is the loss of credibility for many eco-labels. People suspect that the whole thing has been dreamed up by corporate marketing executives far removed from the original intent of eco-labeling.

While eco-labels in other sectors of the economy abound, and recognized and credible guidelines for their development and use are gradually emerging, they are few and far between in tourism. In fact, tourism is relatively new at the business of eco-labeling, and the full impact of existing initiatives is not clearly understood. What we do know is that the state of the art for tourism-specific environmental indicators is still relatively crude and that there is a need to develop site-specific criteria for different types of products and destinations (Iwanowski, 1993). In this regard, the WTO has established an international expert group to tackle this challenge (Manning, 1993). So far, ten core indicators have been identified that would be useful to governments in checking whether a particular operation is doing things right or whether things are seriously wrong. The next step, which is now underway, is to translate these indicators into practical measures that can be readily understood and used to assess the sustainability of site-specific operations (Shackleford, 1994).

## What Makes a Good Eco-Label?

Expressed in very simple terms, what consumers need and want is an understandable and credible eco-labeling system built on the basis of the results of a careful, comprehensive and objective assessment. However, the challenges are immense in developing such schemes. In many past attempts, what appeared to be a black or white process in theory proved to be many shades of gray in practice. Typical issues shaping the credibility and usefulness of these processes include:

- What are the objectives of the scheme? (Encouragement of environmental practice, consumer awareness, product promotion?) (WTTC, 1994)

- What product groups will be covered? (Accommodation, transportation, tours?) This becomes particularly difficult in tourism where product categories are more apt to refer to concepts and notions as opposed to standardized definitions.) (Buckley, 1994)

- What extent of participation by the product group is required? (Is it necessary for all brands in the product group to participate in the system or is it voluntary? Is there a fee for participation? Is the system based on voluntary participation?) (PATA, 1994)

- What differentiation will there be between high and low performers? (Do all participants receive an eco-label? Are there shades of color for eco-labels? Will the process identify progress toward higher standards of performance?) (WTTC, 1993)

- How accessible will the evaluation process be? (What will the evaluation criteria be? How understandable will they be? Will the evaluation results be available for private and/or public scrutiny? Who will establish the criteria?) (Epler Wood, 1993)

- Who will do the evaluation? What are their qualifications/competencies? How credible are self-regulatory systems from the perspective of consumers? Should the evaluators be completely at arm's length from those businesses being assessed? (Gallon, 1992)

## Guidelines for Eco-Labeling Systems

Given the scope of these issues and the experiences of other evaluation schemes, the following guidelines might be useful for developing an eco-labeling system for ecolodges:

- Establish a broad-based approach which identifies general guidelines on the presentation of environmental claims. For example, what uni-

form guidelines can be established to prevent or minimize unscrupulous claims, while promoting truthful and non-deceptive facts about the "greenness" of facilities? Currently some green labels in tourism appear to be awarded for merely claiming to be committed to the philosophy of developing environmentally friendly practices (PATA, 1994).

- Establish an approach which clarifies rules for the use of specific environmental symbols and terms (Chilton, 1991). For example, what requirements must be met before an ecolodge can employ terms related to disposal or waste management alternatives such as "recyclable," "reusable/refillable," "compostable," "degradable," or those related to resource use such as "energy efficient," "water saving." Such rules may assist lodge operators who may need to guide their marketing departments on the meaning and use of environmental terms which are not always easy to express in a few words.

- Establish and promote awareness of the standardized and verifiable testing procedures that are being used to assess the environmental performance of the ecolodge (Epler Wood, 1992). For instance, most tourists are not in a position to test the veracity of many environmental claims that may be associated with an ecolodge. For the most part, they are not on holiday as environmental sleuths or social anthropologists. They may be able to attest to the facility's quality, durability or performance while they are on-site, but are unlikely to be capable of judging whether or not the construction practices associated with the lodge's development were "ecologically sensitive" or "energy efficient." In such instances, it would be worthwhile to have an evaluation system which is clearly transparent to public scrutiny. In the end, the success of an eco-labeling program for tourism depends on getting credible information to the average consumer.

- Establish a system which focuses on encouraging progress beyond mere compliance. Many tourism operators have a stated commitment to promoting environmentally friendly management practices. Most of them are at the beginning of a large learning curve in this regard. A system which identifies strengths and weaknesses and means of improvement will have more value in the long run than one which focuses on rewarding minimum acceptable performance. Many existing labeling systems focus on indicating whether or not a minimum standard has been met. But as members of a larger community of environmentally conscious citizens, tourism operators should want to go beyond simply not being under-achievers and progress to a recognized level of top performance.

## Ecolodge Labeling Criteria

The extent to which an ecolodge can label itself as "environmentally responsible," "earth friendly" or "green" depends to a large extent on the evaluation system used and the criteria of that system. A variety of eco-evaluation systems continues to evolve. These systems center on different dimensions of the environmental management challenge: Creating more sustainable forms of human activity. These include:

- *Ecolodge Development Phases*
  Built on the traditional "stressor activities" associated with most forms of development, these evaluations focus on the extent to which potential environmental impacts are addressed at various stages in the development process. These phases relate to site selection, assessment, planning, design, construction and management (Andersen, 1994).

- *Operational Site Management Practices*
  This approach emphasizes assessing the on-site management practices of facilities as they relate to the use and disposal of solid and liquid wastes (recycling, reusing, composting, reducing) as well as the management of energy resources (water, solar, gas, carbon, etc.). While the focus tends to be placed primarily on on-site management practices, the extent to which environmentally responsible product procurement practices occur might also be included in such evaluations (Hawkes and Williams, 1993).

- *Awareness Building Practices*
  Creating a deeper awareness and commitment among operators, visitors and residents about more sustainable forms of environmental behavior is one of the typical objectives of ecotourism activity. Ecolodges provide a venue for achieving that awareness and resolve. Evaluation criteria might focus on determining the extent to which on-site management focuses on interpretation, education and training for guests, employees, residents, suppliers and the travel industry in general (Buckley, 1994). Evaluation criteria might include an assessment of the extent to which these activities extend into pre- and post-trip programming.

- *Eco-Footprint Management*
  In this approach, the categories of human consumption at an ecolodge could be translated into the areas of productive land needed to provide those items. From that, the area of land required by an ecolodge to provide its resources and assimilate its waste products can be calculated. This measure is known as the ecological footprint of the resort. It is the land that would be required on the planet to support this kind of vacation lifestyle. It identifies how our vacation activities penetrate into the capital asset base of this earth, and it brings the externalities of our leisure lifestyles into focus (Wackernagel, 1993).

## Ecolodge Sustainability Criteria

While all of these approaches provide a possible focus for an evaluation system, the criteria on which they are based emanate from the principles of sustainable development. Our research of the literature and our own investigations suggest that ecolodge tourism should:

- Provide interpretation of natural resources leading to protection and, where appropriate, enhancement of the overall environment;

- ensure that on-site environmentally sensitive cultural resources and processes are left undisturbed, conserved and interpreted;

- sensitively integrate all built structures into the area's natural and cultural environment;

- balance built design with human needs (rather than wants) with carrying capacity of the area's natural and cultural environments;

- increase awareness of energy conservation methods and issues through on-site management practices;

- increase awareness of water conservation methods and issues through management practices;

- increase awareness of solid waste reduction, reuse and recycling methods and issues through on-site management practices;

- increase awareness of biodiversity resource management through on-site management practices;

- support local participation in the stewardship, design development and management of on-site programs and facilities;

- encourage socially appropriate behavior of guests and employees;

- encourage responsible food consumption based on locally and possibly organically grown products, and the use of locally produced and prepared foods;

- encourage product purchasing patterns based on minimum levels of importation, packaging and waste production practices;

- contribute to local protection and community development initiatives;

- participate in environmentally responsible marketing programs (USDI, 1993 and Ecotourism Society, 1993).

## Conclusions

Notwithstanding the potential of developing thoughtful criteria for grading the greenness of tourism facilities, there is one fundamental truth that must be recognized by all tourism's actors. That is, that all products developed for human use have some negative impact on the environment. That impact is largely a function of the way in which the products are produced, transported and used. A product's shade of green as identified on an eco-label really only signifies its environmental friendliness relative to other available products. In the end, while we would all like to believe that our leisure times on vacation are relatively benign, the reality is we don't really have a good appreciation of tourism's true performance in this regard. We need to develop clearer thinking on how to assess the greenness of our tourism activities. Eco-labeling processes might help in that assessment. However, unless such processes are carefully crafted, they may end up only adding to the vast amount of vague, meaningless, unsubstantiated and sometimes downright misleading eco-noise that currently confronts environmentally conscious and frustrated consumers.

*Literature cited:*

Andersen, D.L.A. 1994. "Putting the Pieces Together: Methodology for Site Evaluation and Establishing Sustainable Development Criteria," unpublished paper presented at First International Ecolodge Development Forum and Field Seminar. Maho Bay, U.S. Virgin Islands, October, 1994.

Buckley, R. 1994. "A Framework for Ecotourism," Annals of Tourism Research, Vol. 21(3), pp. 661-665.

Carson, P. and J. Moulden 1991. *Green Is Gold: Business Talking To Business about the Environmental Revolution.* Toronto: Harper Business.

Chilton, D. 1991. "Rules for Green Labeling," Playback Strategy, p. 3.

Clabon, S. 1994. "Ecolabeling," Review of European and International Environmental Law: RECIEL, Vol. 3(1), pp. 21-25.

Ecotourism Society 1993. *Ecotourism Guidelines For Nature Tour Operators.* Bennington, Vermont: The Ecotourism Society.

Environment Canada 1993. Environmental Choice Program. Ottawa: Environment Canada.

Epler Wood, M. 1992. "Defining Criteria for a Consumer Evaluation Program: The Ecotourism Society's National Survey of Outbound Tour Operators," paper presented at World Congress on Adventure Travel and Ecotourism. Colorado Springs: The Adventure Travel Society.

Epler Wood, M. 1993. "Monitoring Ecotourism: are Guidelines Enough?" paper presented at 1993 World Congress on Adventure Travel and Ecotourism. Colorado Springs: The Adventure Travel Society.

Gallon, G. 1992. "The Green Product Endorsement Controversy – Lessons from the Pollution Probe/Loblsaw experience," Alternatives, Vol. 18 (3), pp. 16-25.

Hawkes, S. and P.W. Williams, eds. 1993. *The Greening of Tourism: Principles to Practice*. Burnaby: Centre For Tourism Policy and Research, Simon Fraser University, and Industry, Science and Technology Canada.

Iwanowski, K. 1993. "The Birth of the Ecotel," The Hotel Valuation Journal, October, pp. 1-4.

Lenhart, M. 1994. "Responsible Tourism and the Travel Industry," *Going Green*, supplement to Tour and Travel News, August 29, pp. G. 6-13.

Manning, E.W. 1993. "Managing for Sustainable Tourism: Indicators for Better Decisions," in S. Hawkes and P.W. Williams, eds. *The Greening of Tourism: Principles to Practice*. Burnaby: Centre For Tourism Policy and Research, Simon Fraser University, and Industry, Science and Technology Canada.

Masterton, A.M. 1994. "Sustainable Development: a New Foundation for Tourism Worldwide" *Going Green*, supplement to Tour and Travel News, pp. G14-16.

PATA 1994. "PATA Green Leaf – Symbol of Commitment," Pacific Asia Travel News, Vol. 10, September/October, p. 55.

Strid, S. and N. Carter 1992. "No Free Ride for Eco Ads," *Tomorrow*, pp. 44-50.

Shackleford, P. 1994. "A Global Initiative," *Going Green*, supplement to Tour and Travel News, p. G26.

USDI 1993. "Guiding Principles Of Sustainable Design." Denver: U.S. Department of the Interior.

Valentine, P.S. 1992. "Review, Nature-Based Tourism," in B. Weiler and C.M. Hal, eds. Special Interest Tourism, London: Belhaven, pp. 105-128.

Wacknernagel, M. 1993. *How Big Is Our Ecological Footprint: Using The Concept Of Appropriated Carrying Capacity For Measuring Sustainability*. Vancouver: The Task Force on Planning Healthy and Sustainable Community, University of British Columbia.

Wight, P. 1993. "Ecotourism: Ethics or Ecosell?" Journal of Travel Research, Winter, pp. 3-9.

Williams, P.W. 1993. "Environmental Business Practice: Ethical Codes for Tourism," Arizona Hospitality Trends, Vol. 7 (1), pp. 8-10.

WTTC 1993. *Travel and Tourism: Environment and Development*. Oxford: World Travel and Tourism Environment Research Centre, Oxford Brookes University.

WTTC 1994. *What Is Green Globe?* London: Green Globe Office.

# Environmental Guidelines for the Conventional Lodging Facility

*By Kirk J. Iwanowski*

*"All the initiatives we have put forward have made commercial sense. If we can save energy, we save a lot of money. If we can save water, we save a lot of money. If we reduce waste, we're reducing costs."*

*— John Forte, Forte Plc.*

## Introduction

It is evident from this statement by John Forte, Forte Hotels, Plc. that owners and operators of conventional lodging facilities are realizing the benefits of environmentally sustainable hotel operations. However, given the rampant distribution of information concerning environmental initiatives within the lodging market, many operators are paralyzed by confusion and an abundance of seemingly infinite data. The following discussion will outline the fundamental strategies that a conventional lodging facility should employ in an effort to maximize savings to both the environment and the bottom line. Environmental initiatives no longer carry the same price tag or reputation for negatively impacting the guest experience that may have been true five years ago. Today, significant cost savings can be realized through a concentration on five basic areas of operation: Solid waste management and recycling, water conservation, energy efficiency, legislative compliance and employee environmental education and training.

## Starting From Square One

Please note that the following operational guidelines are designed to apply to the conventional lodging facility – a hotel property not originally constructed with the issues of conservation and preservation in mind. Secondly, as a hotel property – as opposed to another form of commercial establishment – the building contains tens, hundreds and perhaps thousands of guest rooms that are designed to function in a number of capacities, including office space, temporary homes and vacation getaways. Each guest room, although a component of the main building, must give the illusion of being totally self-contained. Unlike most other office buildings and commercial spaces, the hotel must function 24 hours a day, 365 days a year. Finally, the primary focus of the operation is to provide the highest standard of service consistent with the market segment it serves. It is only with these considerations in mind that the hotel operator can be sure of developing a comprehensive environmental program that not only incorporates the operational policies and requirements of the property but also never compromises the guest experience.

Before program development begins, it is essential to meet the following fundamental principles:

- *Guarantee executive level commitment:* The general manager and the executive committee should act as the example and serve as a source of support in participating in and promoting the property-level environmental program. The line staff will constantly be looking to the top for guidance and feedback and, as the example, the hotel executives need to be willing and available to provide it. In addition, it is essential that the general manager establish the environmental program as a priority throughout the daily operation of the hotel; the hotel staff will be testing to see if "things have really changed."

- *Place an individual in charge of each "primary" aspect of the program:* Individuals with the knowledge, time and motivation to spearhead the major sections of the campaign (recycling, energy management, education and so forth) should be selected. Implicit in this position should be the responsibility and authority to make any program modifications.

- *Develop a "Green Team":* This team should be comprised of the hotel general manager and executive committee members, the program directors and select representatives from each department, including managers and line employees. The responsibility of this committee is to seek, generate and help implement new aspects of the environmental program.

- *Continually monitor performance:* At the onset, establish benchmarks for tracking progress regularly. Schedule a periodic review of the environmental program to evaluate employee performance, calculate cost savings to date and make any modifications. The staff should be

provided with regular updates on their progress and accomplishments to maintain levels of motivation.

If these factors are in place, the hotel operator should begin to consider the development of a systematic approach to the management of environmental issues. Systematic in this context refers to those elements of the operation central to the facility and consistent across hotel departments. The three elements of an environmental program associated with the most significant potential for cost savings and immediate return on investment are solid waste management and recycling, water conservation and energy efficiency.

## Solid Waste Management and Recycling

Solid waste management and disposal is an expense linked directly to a property's profit and loss statement. If a property can reduce the volume of trash produced, the frequency of pick-up is lowered, thus decreasing monthly hauling fees. Given the rate at which local landfills and dumps are closing, and the volume of waste generated by a single hotel property every day, it comes as no surprise that there are significant savings in diverting major waste components from the solid waste stream. However, contrary to popular belief, recycling is only one component of a solid waste management program and should be the final alternative to disposal. Before recycling, efforts to reduce and reuse waste and product should be exhausted.

To produce optimum results in reducing waste and saving dollars, you must carry out the following tasks:

1. Identify all activities and locations throughout the operation that generate waste.

2. Analyze the waste stream – identify the major components of trash produced including glass, paper, plastic, cardboard, organic matter and so forth.

3. Evaluate local regulations and county ordinances for recycling and waste treatment and disposal; evaluate health and fire codes.

4. Evaluate the market for recycled products – what is the demand by haulers, waste

exchangers and charity organizations for specific components of the waste stream?

5. Select a waste hauler.

   • If the city does not collect certain materials, identify a network of private local haulers who will collect the material.

   • Determine if it is more cost effective to use only one waste hauler.

   • Identify which materials are recyclables.

   • How should recycled materials be collected – separated or mixed?

   • Identify the a minimum volume or weight for pick-up by the hauler.

   • Does the hauler provide or lease disposal and/or recycling collection equipment? What is provided? What is the cost?

   • What is the cost of hauling the recyclable materials?

   • Does the hauler provide educational materials to promote the recycling program?

   • Will the hauler provide assistance in program design based on volume produced?

   • Will the hauler track volume statistics on materials reclaimed?

6. Determine space, container and equipment needs based on the constraints of the facility and local operating environment.

7. Develop an action plan.

   • Create a written program.

   • Include specific goals and objectives that take into account local regulations.

   • Expand the program gradually; set 2- and 4-year objectives.

   • Design the system to allow for interdepartmental flexibility; take a systematic approach.

   • Identify how you will monitor the success of the program – frequency of hauling, volume, etc.

8. Combine efforts with neighboring businesses. It is not uncommon for haulers to dictate mandatory levels of volume for recycled materials collection. If your property does not meet these levels, coordinate collection with a neighboring business to meet volume requirements.

9. Create a user-friendly recycling program.

   • Clearly label collection containers with designated material types and contaminants.

   • Translate labels into all languages represented on property.

   • Provide a sufficient number of containers in convenient locations.

10. Monitor progress and provide feedback.

   • Use comparative impact studies to illustrate staff accomplishments.

   • Provide a suggestion/recommendation box.

The benefits of a hotel-wide solid waste management program are far-reaching. Aside from a decrease in operating costs through the reduction of waste generation, consider the opportunities to offset additional costs such as frequent product or equipment replacement or the inadvertent disposal of reusable products (count how much silverware, china and linen is mistakenly thrown away throughout the property; quantify the savings that would be realized through closer monitoring of waste disposal). Secondly, by incorporating a comprehensive waste program, you are in a position to anticipate impending regulations for recycling and reclamation and avoid costly fines for non-compliance. Finally, consider the operational benefits of such a program through increased levels of awareness by the hotel staff and the sense of pride and ownership that occurs.

## Water Conservation

Each year it takes more than two million gallons of water to feed, clothe and bathe a single U.S. citizen. Also, Americans use approximately 450 billion gallons of water each day. Is it any surprise that water conservation techniques are among the measures most frequently employed by hotel properties? In an effort to construct your water conservation program, consider the following factors:

1. What is the condition of the local water supply? Is there a drought?

2. Obtain past and current water consumption patterns and meter readings at the property level.

3. Contact the local municipality or water authority to determine if any rebate or conservation programs are offered for reduction of water consumption.

4. Inventory water-consuming equipment currently in place. Are conservation tactics employed? Is replacement or retrofit an option?

Water conservation tactics can be readily incorporated into the following components of your lodging establishment:

Showers
(low-flow shower heads: 2.5 gallons per minute)

Toilets
(low-flow toilets: 1.5-1.6 gallons per flush; infrared sensors)

Urinals
(Sloan valve replacements 1.0-1.6 gallons per flush; infrared sensors)

Sinks
(aerators: 11,700 gallons per year; infrared sensors)

Irrigation equipment

Water features
(pools, decorative fountains and so forth)

## Energy Efficiency

There are several factors inherent in hotel operations that influence energy consumption throughout the building: Weather, occupancy rates, programs and activities run by the hotel, thermostats in individual guest rooms, equipment selection, cleaning and maintenance schedules and the size, condition, age and location of property. These are all characteristics of hotel operations; thus, they must all be factored into the equation which determines energy efficiency. According to Chervenack, Keane & Company and American Hotel & Motel Association (AH&MA) technology consultants, the energy expense of American hotels represents 5.2% of the industry's $40 billion in gross revenues, or an annual $2 billion energy expense. With such a significant percentage of revenues being spent on energy, an analysis of your property's engineering and maintenance facilities from an energy conservation standpoint may prove to be time – as opposed to dollars – well spent.

The objectives of the energy conservation program include:

1. Identifying how the property's equipment and actual facility consume energy.

2. Creating a short- and long-term plan to increase levels of efficiency.

3. Determining how the hotel can increase the life of the equipment currently in use, and how to incorporate equipment retrofits to reduce energy consumption.

4. Identifying the problem consumtion areas within the hotel.

5. Analyzing how the hotel can directly reduce operating costs through reduced consumption.

Before the design and implementation of the energy management program, consider the following issues:

• Has the property undergone an energy audit or consultation by a private firm, local utility or state agency during the past three years of operation?

• Is a formal energy conservation program currently in place? Has it been formally communicated to all hotel employees? How?

• Is a system in place to track utility and energy consumption data? Is this used to determine what areas of the property are light and heavy consumers?

• Has a preventive maintenance program been implemented by the engineering department?

• Is the hotel staff trained and encouraged to practice energy conservation through workshops and incentive programs?

• Is energy conservation incorporated into the employee training and orientation program?

• Is a system in place to keep staff informed about the latest in energy conservation and efficient practices?

- Is the hotel equipment currently in use energy efficient? Obtain the manufacturers' guidelines and recommendations for all equipment used on property.

To begin the development of the program:
- Collect all existing data on energy consumption patterns over a period of three years. Use this information to create a data reference to track consumption and cost over time.

- Record and analyze price and consumption data to identify patterns related to season, department, etc.

- Compare your findings to the standard efficiency benchmarks for properties consistent with your market segment; use these benchmarks to create goals for the property.

- Educate yourself on the specifics of the building and its environment (geographic locations, surrounding buildings, site conditions, monthly degree days, etc.).

- Obtain and review equipment plan and layout.

- Form an energy conservation committee, including the general manager, director of engineering and a representative from each of the major departments.

- List and prioritize all no-cost, low-cost and capital expenditures to improve energy conservation and cost reduction. Propose an action plan that objectively evaluates any measure considered to be a capital investment. Arrange the list from least to longest payback time and quantify all potential returns, when possible.

- Design an action plan for each department and set tentative completion deadlines.

- The program should consider all energy consuming equipment; most important are:
  - Heating, ventilation and air conditioning throughout the property:
    gas furnaces
    package terminal air conditioners (PTACs)
    fan coils
    baseboards
    window air conditioner units

    heat pumps
  - Exhaust and ventilation systems include:
    central systems
    rooftop package units
    air handlers
    variable-air-volume (VAV)
    heat recovery systems
    evaporative cooling
    steam condensate

When reviewing lighting issues, regardless of whether a total replacement or retrofit is to be conducted, consider several automated controls on the lighting system to reduce superfluous lighting throughout the property:
- Timers: Use these in low-traffic areas, smaller spaces, and non-guest contact areas.

- Photo Controls: Extremely effective for exterior lamping to regulate light output according to exterior light levels.

- Occupancy sensors: Use in low-traffic areas, primarily non-guest contact areas.

According to one of the leading U.S.-based energy consulting firms, Xenergy Inc., lighting used to be designed with aesthetics and low first cost as the primary considerations. However, given the recent rise of electricity costs, operators are beginning to realize the benefits of energy efficient lighting because of the lower operating costs of the most widely used fixtures. While incandescent lighting has a low first cost, it is only one-fourth as efficient as fluorescent and one-sixth as efficient as metal halide lighting, thus requiring four and six times more electricity, respectively, to produce a given amount of light.

However, as part of determining the efficiency of a given light fixture, one has to consider three specific issues of the hotel environment:

1. Color: Incandescent and fluorescent light types produce different color renditions, due to differing temperature levels. Incandescent lamps (2700-3000K) produce a soft white or yellow light while fluorescents (2700-3500K) produce a whiter light effect. This is an extremely important aesthetics and safety con-

sideration; desired light levels vary according to the location of the fixture and purpose of the space which it illuminates.

2. Lamp Design: The installation of fluorescent lamps requires new fixtures and special ballasts (electric being the most efficient); capital availability is an issue.

3. Life: While fluorescents are more expensive than incandescents, fluorescent and metal halide fixtures last ten to fifteen times longer than incandescent fixtures.

## Keys to Success

Creating and implementing a hotel environmental program is property-specific. Many aspects of hotel operations are dictated or limited by the property's environment. While this is an individual effort, there are six keys to success that the operator should remember when developing and implementing the environmental program:

- Maintain a comprehensive approach: To maximize the return on investment of an environmental initiative while developing a program with the greatest potential to impact the consumption of natural resources, address the three fundamental issues of waste management, water conservation and energy efficiency. With these three elements as the core of the hotel environmental program, you are taking a systems approach to the management of environmental issues. Again, a system is defined here as an operating issue that is not unique to only one area or department of the hotel, but rather is an operational concern within the guest room and throughout both the public and back-of-house space.

- Use engineering-based strategies: Given the recent explosion of data on energy conservation, rebate programs, water consumption and quality, lighting retrofits and so forth, many operators felt too confused to implement an engineering-based environmental program. From a cost standpoint, it is not until the property-level envi-

ronmental program takes an engineering approach that the potential for significant savings can be realized. Thus, many operators are discovering that it is more efficient to develop a program that emphasizes a balance between engineering- and equipment-based strategies, as well as operational tactics.

- Include departmental tactics: It is essential that the environmental program incorporate each operational department within the hotel to maximize the impact of the environmental initiative. Each department has specific functions and responsibilities; as a result, the environmental program should be modified by department to reflect the activities performed in each. Given the scope of a conventional lodging facility, the following departments should be addressed in the program:

  Rooms
  Food and beverage
  Meetings and banquets
  Guest rooms
  Housekeeping
  Administrative offices
  Purchasing
  Receiving/garbage/general storage areas
  Engineering
  Building envelope

- Incorporate the eco-program into standard operating procedure: The objective of the environmental initiative is to incorporate the fundamental principles of environmentalism into standard operating procedure. Conventional hotel programs tend to be short-term and met with initial enthusiasm which rapidly declines. By avoiding the "program mentality" and incorporating new strategies and tactics into daily practice, chances for long-term success are strengthened. An internal departmental audit must be conducted to determine how current standard operating procedure should be modified to incorporate the environmental objectives detailed in the initiative.

- Employee training and education: Effective training and education of hotel employees is paramount to the success of the property-level environmental program. The executive committee, middle managers and line employees must be fully knowledgeable about the purpose and specifics of the environmental program before it can be put into practice. Even though the emphasis of the environmental program is on an engineering- or systems-based approach, the equipment is only as effective as the people who use it. Only when the proper systems and behavior are in place can the benefits of an environmental program be maximized.

• Clear communication: Once the environmental program has been implemented throughout the property, market its presence to employees and guests to raise levels of awareness and motivation. Marketing efforts to the guest should be deliberate and specific in order to avoid any confusion or misconceptions. Travelers are increasingly skeptical about hotels' environmental claims; make your objectives clear in an environmental mission or policy statement that details the strategies that have been employed to reduce consumption of energy and water and the generation of waste. Analyze existing marketing vehicles from brochures to key passports and modify their layout to include your environmental message.

savings typically results from a program that addresses three fundamental issues: Solid waste management and recycling, water conservation and energy efficiency. These three operational issues transcend department and provide a framework for the development of a comprehensive hotel-wide environmental program.

## Conclusion

The majority of hotel properties and lodging establishments in use today were not originally constructed with environmental sustainability in mind. However, this does not preclude the systematic implementation of strategies designed to decrease the consumption of natural resources for the conventional lodging establishment.

The fundamental principles of environmentalism are tied to issues of efficiency. An efficient lodging operation minimizes its consumption of natural resources not only to conserve the resources themselves but also to reduce the costs of their consumption. Given the nature of a conventional lodging facility, the greatest environmental impact and potential for

# Chapter 6:

# Ecolodge Case Studies

# The Conservation Corporation —
## Development and Management of Ecolodging in Africa

*By Alan Bernstein*

## The Conservation Corporation – Conservation Development

The Conservation Corporation ("ConsCorp") was established in 1990 to develop the potential of the ecotourism industry in southern Africa – in accordance with sound conservation principles. The operating ethic of the group is based on a commitment to care – care of the land, care of wildlife and care of people (that is, guests, local communities and staff). The group believes that this commitment to care will ensure that the wilderness areas it manages will remain economically viable and ecologically sustainable in the long term.

## Phinda Forest Lodge

At the Phinda Forest Lodge in Northern Zululand, South Africa, ConsCorp was faced with developing in an ecologically fragile forest on sandy soils in an inaccessible, hot and humid area whose local communities had been largely cut off from economic development for many decades. These factors provided unique opportunities for the project.

First, "clean" construction was essential, requiring a minimum of concrete and wet trades. Because of delicate sandy founding conditions, buildings had to be raised above ground level on slender hand-augured piles. To avoid encroaching on the forest canopy, a low-pitch roofing system was required, and this precluded the traditional gum pole and thatch construction which typifies African safari lodges.

To ensure that a developed world standard of construction could be delivered by largely unskilled local workers at a competitive price, extensive use was made of pre-fabricated, shop-fitted elements manufactured in South Africa's urban centers; on-site work was limited to fairly simple construction procedures. In effect, the design and construction process which evolved at the Phinda Forest Lodge removed the complexity from the on-site construction process and transferred it to locations where the relevant skills existed.

The completed lodge consists of 16 rooms, each forming a secluded glass and wood enclave, and a central lounge, dining and pool area nestled into the edge of the Southern Maputaland Sand Forest in Northern Zululand, South Africa.

To ensure minimum disruption of or damage to the forest and its ecology, but maximum economic input by local communities, ConsCorp founded a construction company, Phinda Construction, to upgrade skills and provide employment in the area. It employed 110 local unskilled people on the project, with only four skilled craftsmen being imported to assist and supervise. The emphasis was on minimal mechanization; the construction of each unit was simplified with a type of composite construction using concrete bricks, concrete columns and beams and timber. The entire finished floor of each unit is suspended above the ground, and permanent scaffold-jacks were used to eliminate any alignment problems. Internal floors were constructed primarily out of raised timber decking and suspended floor joists with tiled floors in bathrooms.

The Conservation Corporation completed the US$2 million Forest Lodge without uprooting a single tree and virtually without importing any construction skills from outside the Phinda area. As a result, over US$1 million was injected into these remote, rural communities and several small businesses were created in the process (e.g., transport and brick making). Quantity surveyors estimate that conventional construction processes and contracts procedures would have added approximately US$1 million to the project cost.

The key to success in developing the Phinda

Forest Lodge in this way lay in the time and attention we devoted to the planning and design stage. The design conceptualization and refinement process lasted from August 1992 to March 1993. During this time, each element of the building was carefully researched and designed, and the Phinda Construction company was slowly assembled with a close focus on the type of resources, construction management procedures and general infrastructure which would ultimately be required after construction started.

Under the guidance of the newly appointed lodge leader, the construction crew was gradually assembled from the Phinda Resource Reserve communities – drawn from people who had a deep knowledge of the area and had been involved in habitat management, game management or other aspects of existing hospitality services.

Finally, the Phinda Forest Lodge team, the design concept and the construction method were put to the test by building a full-scale prototype room in the forest. This proved to be an essential part of the development process and we were able to identify fundamental changes needed in the design, the construction method and the make-up of the construction team and its subcontractor relationships.

In late May, 1993, the Phinda Forest Lodge construction began in earnest. The lodge received its first guest on October 10, 1993 – barely six months after the construction started.

Within a month of completion, the Phinda Forest Lodge entered its first high season and was running at almost 100% occupancy – and the fact that the construction of a fine lodge, by approximately 150 people in an area of no more than 4 acres, was barely noticeable.

## Investing in Sustainable Ecotourism Development

The Conservation Corporation has developed a model for conservation development in Africa which is based on an integrated approach to tourism, conservation, rural venture capital investment and development. Our investment and development experiences have evolved several principles which have become central to our philosophies for doing business in Africa.

First, the capital and infrastructural requirements for developing in the remote, rural parts of Africa require a long-term investment approach. This implies a high proportion of equity funding, with the corollary of producing appropriately high rates of return on funds employed to account for the business and political risk of making an equity investment in Africa.

Second, the Conservation Corporation does not seek to own (or consider it appropriate that private sector corporations should own) wildlife land in Africa. Our approach is therefore to create partnerships with the regional governments and local communities. Security of tenure is obtained via long-term use agreements, with the resulting rental, lease and traversing fees flowing directly to the local communities. The partnership principles extend throughout our corporate structures.

Over the years, ConsCorp's lodges have evolved within a readily discernible economic profile. A typical 40-60 bed ConsCorp lodge in Africa:

- Costs approximately US$50,000 per bed to develop (with approximately US$1.8 million spent in the local region);

- achieves US$300 per person per night (or approximately US$1.3 million per annum of cash flow through the local communities);

- operates at 70-75% occupancy after 2 to 3 years (and so sustains 1,500 to 4,000 people in the local area);

- employs 150-200 rural people;

- uses 15,000 hectares of wild land;

- produces an internal rate of return of 25% to 30%.

The Conservation Corporation hopes to continue developing a sustainable, viable ecotourism industry in Africa, based on the low density (but high economic yield) principles set out in this paper.

# The Futuro Model Rainforest Lodge
# IICT Training Academy
# Native Crafts Center
## A Demonstration Project of Sustainable Ecotourism

*By Michael M.S. Chun*

In recent years, the plight of the great rainforests of the Amazon basin in Brazil has evoked worldwide concern. These immense forests, storehouses of unimaginable biological richness, have been imperiled by traditional slash and burn agriculture, logging, cattle grazing, mining and other exploitative practices.

Individuals, local communities, environmental groups, government agencies and corporations have espoused ecotourism as one possible solution to the forests' degradation. Ecotourism at its best would seem to merge the interests of a rapidly growing segment of the tourist population with a conservation ethic, the possibility of profit for various segments of the tourism industry and a sustainable livelihood for local inhabitants.

FUTURO/IICT, a non-profit association of corporate, academic and government entities, proposes to design, build, manage and maintain a working model for sustainable nature tourism which demonstrates low-impact design; use of native ingenuity, labor, materials and construction techniques; and state-of-the-art energy resources and waste disposal technologies. In order for the lodge/academy/crafts center to serve as a model of excellence for ecotourism development in the Amazon basin, it must also demonstrate that such a project can succeed financially.

The model lodge/training academy/crafts center project is a joint undertaking between Foundation for the Future (FUTURO), which will oversee design, development and construction, and Instituto

Interamericano de Capacitacion Turistica (IICT), which will develop and administer educational programs and manage operations of the various components. All profits from the FUTURO/IICT model project will be directed into its educational programs and conservation efforts in the region.

Sustainable development mandates a balance of socioeconomic growth with the natural resources of a particular area; the human community of the Amazon basin, their economic well-being and the preservation of their traditions must be considered as an integral, essential part of the natural community.

The proposed project will promote a more diversified economy based on educating neighboring inhabitants for jobs in the rapidly growing local ecotourism industry, in sustainable forestry and in nature education. It will also work to create jobs in the production and marketing of native handicrafts.

One of the three central components of the project is the Rainforest Lodge. This readily adaptable, unintrusive facility will reflect precise study and detailed knowledge of local climate conditions and understanding of performance characteristics of local building materials.

In this way, the model lodge will incorporate the pragmatic sagacity of the indigenous people into a state-of-the art, sustainable design by the international architectural firm Wimberly Allison Tong & Goo. The small lodge will provide exceptional accommodations which allow visitors to enjoy the rainforest from a vantage point set well above the ground for views, privacy, natural ventilation and flood control. Verandas are on three sides of each unit; all services and utilities will be hidden under pathways. A central dining/lounge/interpretive center will be the social and educational hub of the guest area. The surrounding forest is the central focus of the lodge design and of the complementary design of the nearby academy, its dormitory facilities and the arts and crafts work/display center.

Part of the difficulty in establishing a responsible ecotourism project is in finding the means to retain profit within the host country and region. The educational arm of the proposed model is an innovative on-site training and exchange program developed by IICT to meet the need for additional and alternative work opportunities for the people of the Brazilian Amazon region.

IICT, using the facilities and in-place programs of Hocking Technical College, has devised a curriculum of applied training to increase employment opportunities and to promote a healthier environment in an area where there has been a rapid surge of ecotourism interest and development.

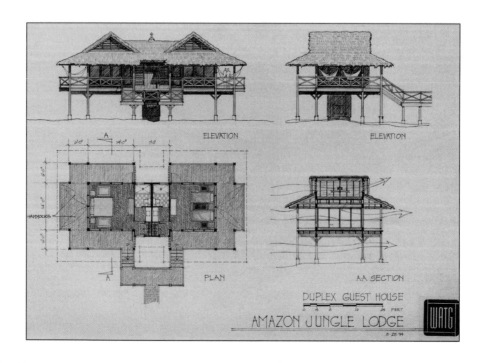

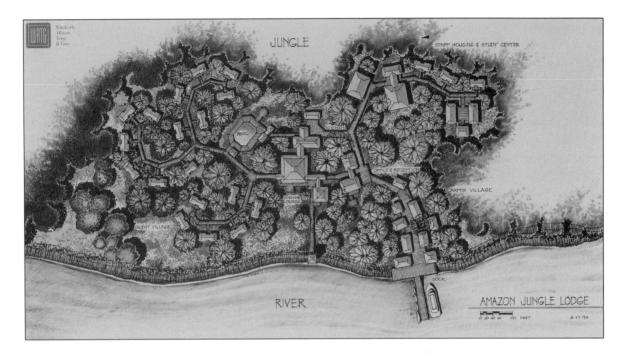

The IICT Academy will include comprehensive programs in travel and tourism, culinary arts, hotel/restaurant management and maintenance, and in natural resources technology with emphasis in forestry management and ranger interpretive/protective services.

IICT will employ Brazilian teachers and will offer Brazilian students opportunities to visit the Ohio campus where on-site resources include a nature center, a 400-acre wildlife management laboratory and a full-service, on-site motel facility.

As tourism moves in, local inhabitants are often pushed out. This part of the proposed model project will help stem migration to crowded urban areas of Brazil as it affords varied opportunities in newly opening ecolodges and the surrounding wilderness areas.

The IICT Academy will also offer compelling educational opportunities to guests of the lodge as part of their experience of the rainforest. Educational forums, roundtable discussion groups and small studio and field workshops will challenge and illuminate perceptions on such subjects as biodiversity and two of the most important activities sustaining life on earth: Pollination and photosynthesis. In a chautauqua-like setting, demonstration and participatory classes will feature such subjects as native cookery, botanical pharmaceuticals and local folklore employing native teachers to stimulate interest, strengthen understanding and encourage guests' active participation in protection of

the rainforest ecosystem.

The third component of the FUTURO/IICT project is an on-site outlet for the demonstration and sale of native handicrafts. This crafts center showcase will help revive traditional cultural practices that are beginning to disappear and, at the same time, introduce another means of livelihood to nearby villages through the sale of craft items to guests and to day visitors arriving at the boat dock. Craft activities will be selected through recommendations of indigenous peoples. Materials used will be chosen and managed to sustain, rather than deplete, local resources.

For many decades, the vast Amazon basin has offered a seemingly limitless opportunity for destructive exploitation. Today the results of those ventures threaten the well-being of Brazil and of the entire world. It is time to replace short-sighted profit motivation with far-sighted vision. A standard for excellence in responsible ecotourism facility and program design is an international imperative. A coherent, constructive, proactive program which creates a model of sustainability can reverse a situation of profound ecological crisis to one of increased economic stability and environmental gain for all.

# "AMAZZONIA '90"
## A New Tourism Approach in the Amazon

The lives of indigenous peoples in the Amazon of Brazil have been greatly disrupted by the coming of industrialization. Cities have lured them from the forest and rivers with the promise of work, yet most are trapped in the marginalized existence in the poverty-stricken suburbs known as favelas.

For some years, volunteers have worked hard to stem the exodus, in some cases even creating agricultural schools to teach essential farming skills in order to keep people on the land. Developing local resources – cultural and natural – with the help of local people seemed the most effective way to slow the departure of so many to the difficult life that faced them in the favelas.

It was in this context that the Italian cooperative, Amazzonia '90, was born. With ecotourism spreading greatly in popularity, the cooperative's solution was to develop a nature-based holiday village 80 kilometers from Manaus on a small branch of Rio Negro, one of the Amazon's largest tributaries. Known for its brown, tannin-rich waters that repel mosquitoes, Rio Negro is seldom used for navigation and would ensure quiet stays for visitors to the village. In addition, between the village and Manaus is the famous archipelago of Anavilhanas which, with its 360 islands, is one of the great marvels of the Amazon region.

The financing of the village came from cooperative shareholders of modest means in Modena, Italy, who were motivated to aid poor people in another country. Minimum contributions were priced at US$300, while those who could contribute a minimum of US$2,000 would be entitled to spend one free week at the village each year. By the end of 1994, more than 1,300 Italians had bought shares in the cooperative. As a statement of support for the project, the state government of Brazil donated the large parcel of land.

Construction of the village was begun in 1992 by local builders trained in their crafts by members of Amazzonia '90. Only local, unendangered materials were used. Designed in a horsehoe to simulate the shape of Indian tents known as malocas, the village will house a reception and lounge area, swimming pool, gardens, a restaurant and kitchen, a 200-seat conference room and comfortable, cool lodging rooms – each with a veranda – to house up to 150 visitors. The village functions primarily as a base for ecotourist activity led by trained local guides in the forest and on the rivers. Full-scale activity is expected to begin sometime in 1995.

Once the project is underway, the local population will be able to remain on the land in their original environment, thus reducing the exodus to the cities and safeguarding the environment. Profits from the operation of the village will then be designated for humanitarian and social projects in Manaus. Much of this work will take the form of training for a wide variety of vocational and service occupations. The cooperative also intends to help create schools and daycare centers in the favelas, hostels for street kids, kindergartens, consumer cooperatives, medical clinics, micro enterprises for youngsters and businesses to export Brazilian handcrafted products.

– Giovanni Pradelli, Sara Carraro

# The Grand Bwa Lodge and Wilderness Resort
## Commonwealth of Dominica, Windward Islands, Eastern Caribbean

*By Douglas White*

LODGE ELEVATION

*"The Grand Bwa or high woods are those tracts of virgin forest that still cover much of the island's mountainous interior. . . . It is here that the gigantic Gommiers, Carapite and Bois Diable reach their full majesty."*
                    – Our Island Culture *by Lennox Honychurch*

The Grand Bwa Lodge and Wilderness Resort (pronounced Grand Bw AH) is a proposed upscale, high-quality 50-room ecotourism hotel. Guests can enjoy the splendor of Dominica's natural beauty from the lodge's 43 acres of lush mountain vegetation. The site, 2000 feet above the Caribbean Sea, has two streams, a waterfall and small river. It is adjacent to the Morne Trois Pitons National Forest with dramatic views of the 4550-foot-high Pitons to the south and Dominica's highest peak, Morne Diablotin (4747 feet) to the north.

The resort will stress preservation of the natural environment in a balanced relationship between development and environmental conservation. Sustainable development practices and renewable energy concepts are major components in this holistic approach to tropical resort design. These concepts are used in all aspects of infrastructure development, site planning, environmental restoration and landscaping, materials selection, architectural design and facility management.

Grand Bwa will provide facilities for small conferences, cultural and environmental seminars, exhibitions, crafts workshops and organic gardening demonstrations. Daily nature walks within the resort property, "back of the house" renewable energy infrastructure workshops and excursions into Dominica's extensive National Park System will be offered.

The resort will be divided into three general areas: Grand Bwa Lodge and Cabins, Grand Bwa Village and Grand Bwa Organic Farm and Botanical Gardens. Ten acres along the river will remain undisturbed, except for hiking trails.

## Infrastructure Development Guidelines

- Preservation of the site through minimum site disturbance. Structures will be located only in second growth vegetation areas previously cleared for agriculture. All primal forest areas will be undisturbed;

- emphasis on the use of local Caribbean resources; e.g., materials and craftsmanship;

- a holistic approach to infrastructure development whereby all aspects of infrastructure are seen as interdependent;

- use of renewable energy resources – hydro, wind and solar power;

- emphasis on sewage as a recyclable resource rather than a disposal problem;

- emphasis on the use of recyclable and recycled products and materials;

- use of self-contained DIET (Design Integrated Environmental Technology) buildings for the cabins to minimize site disturbance for mechanical and electrical system lines throughout the site;

- simplicity of design, use of quality materials, low-maintenance systems.

### A Holistic Approach to Infrastructure Development

The site has an elevation change over its length of approximately 300 feet. A spring and two streams run from the top of the site to a small river along the bottom boundary. Water will be taken from the river at the bottom with ram lift pumps, which operate on water pressure differential, without an outside power source. The ram pumps will pump the river water up 300 feet where it will be stored in cisterns above the resort. It will be gravity fed for use throughout the resort. Wastewater from the resort will be processed biologically through two bioconversion systems to return the water to tertiary condition. It will be

dropped back down 300 feet to a hydro generator to produce electricity as it is returned to the river flow in a pure condition.

### Waste Bioconversion Systems

Although Dominica has 365 rivers and "plenty" of water (it actually exports water), low-flush 1.5 gallon toilets will be used to minimize sewage generation. Two different bioconversion systems have been designed to purify and recycle the waste on site. The individual rooms, or cabins, will have WET (Wolverton Environmental Treatment) systems. Dr. Bill Wolverton has designed a plant-based ecological biofilter system for each of the hotel rooms. These odorless systems are essentially small-scale constructed wetland lined planter beds that will be built around and below each unit. The sewage flows directly into these planters where it is purified first by anaerobic digestion and then by the microbes attached to the roots of the plants. The system produces tertiary water that will be added to the resort return flow into the river, through the hydro generator. These systems were originally developed at NASA for future space stations on Mars. They are economical to construct, contain no moving parts, require no energy to operate and eliminate the need for a central sewage collection and pumping system.

The lodge and village areas will employ a McElvaney Associates Bioconversion system. This system will accept sewage, vegetable and organic kitchen waste, landscape and agricultural waste, paper and cardboard products. These are all passed through a grinder into an anaerobic digestor. The system produces methane gas, organic fertilizer and tertiary water. The methane gas will be used to power refrigeration systems (kitchens, administrative offices, etc.) and alternative vehicles. The refrigeration systems will also have heat exchangers to produce hot water. The organic fertilizer will be used in the farm or sold to local farmers. The tertiary water will be dropped back down to the hydro generator to produce electricity and returned to the river.

### Renewable Energy Systems

Grand Bwa will be powered by hydro, solar and wind power. The hydroelectric generator will use a 6-inch diameter sluice with a 300-foot head. The water

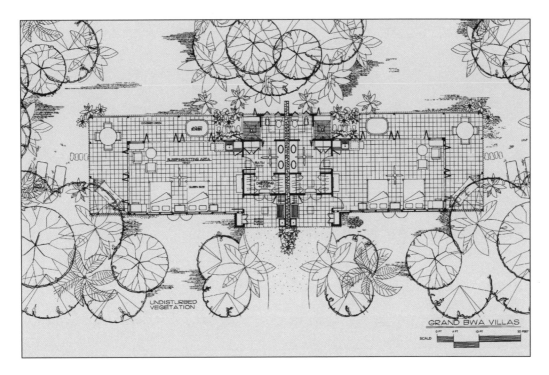

UNDISTURBED
VEGETATION

GRAND BWA VILLAS

source will be the stream on-site combined with tertiary wastewater from the resort. Photovoltaic panels
and solar hot water heaters will also be integral with
each roof structure of the cabins. Large wind turbines
will provide power for the village and will be intercon-
nected to Dominica's hydroelectric power grid.

*Facility Management*

On the operations side of the facility, a minimal use of
plastic and aerosol products will be emphasized.
Reusable and recycled packaging and minimization of
the use of disposable products will be standard procedure. For example, there will be no disposable plastic
utensils or plates packed in picnic lunches for hikes
into the rainforest. Green rooms and handicapped
accessibility will be standards for resort design.

It is envisioned that "back of the house tours"
will also be an important part of the resort program.
People will want to tour the renewable energy and
bioconversion systems.

## Resort Architecture: Sustainable
## Tropical Design

A reverence for nature and integration within the natural Caribbean environment will be the dominant
architectural themes. I believe that for too many years
architects have focused on separating man from nature
within the built environment. Architects must now
turn their attention to reuniting man with nature and
natural biosystems.

Design Integration Environmental Technology
(DIET) buildings have their own structurally integrated biological operating systems. They contain systems
to generate power with building-integrated photovoltaics, produce hot water, collect and store rainwater, maximize the use of day lighting and purify waste
with ecological biofilters. These systems are all integrated into, not added onto, the architecture.

Resort guests will want to experience the
ambiance and special character of Dominica and the
Caribbean. The cabins combine traditional West
Indian vernacular architectural elements with DIET
building concepts. Grand Bwa's architecture also
incorporates unique elements of Caribbean design,
such as the free flow of interior and exterior spaces.

Local materials and craftspeople will be employed
throughout the project. The dominant materials will
be stone and native wood, harvested locally, through
sustainable forestry methods monitored by the World
Wildlife Fund. The overall ambiance of the lodge will
reflect the local architecture of a Caribbean great
house juxtaposed with the interior warmth of a mountain cabin.

The resort cabins will be extremely spacious and comfortable. They will be open to nature on two sides with the use of sliding and folding shutter walls. Each unit will have locally made antique mahogany four poster beds, a sitting and reading area, walk-in closets, indoor/outdoor shower. A hot water soaking tub will be recessed into covered decks that surround each unit.

Dominica has an extensive furniture building industry for a small Caribbean island. Most of the furniture used in the resort will be locally produced and patterned from the government's extensive collection of Caribbean antiques. All furnishings and interior design will highlight the best of Caribbean crafts traditions. All furniture, pottery, baskets and culinary items that are locally produced will also be available in the gift shop.

## Transportation

The lodge and cabins will be accessible only by solar/electric/alternative fuel vehicles. No automobiles will be allowed to enter the forest area. A transfer lounge and parking area will be built just outside the forest in an area previously cleared for agriculture.

## Grand Bwa Village

The activity center of the resort will be located on a knoll with dramatic, sweeping views of the valley. It will provide services for the general public as well as resort guests. The primary elements of the village are seminar and meeting rooms, restaurant and bar and an open-air (covered) small amphitheater for cultural shows and lectures. Boutiques, craft workshops and fruit, vegetable and flower vendors will be located around an open plaza. The village will be complete with covered pedestrian walkways linking it to landscaped parking areas. Arts and crafts, cultural and nature programs and activities will be centered in the village.

## Grand Bwa Organic Farm and Botanical Gardens

Organic farming techniques will be used in cultivating fruits and vegetables for the resort on a portion of the site previously cleared for agriculture. Additionally the Grand Bwa Farms will support a small cottage industry to produce local food products. Homemade hot sauce, spices, teas and jams will be used in the resort and sold in the gift shop. Guests will be encouraged to participate in cooking and gardening programs. The

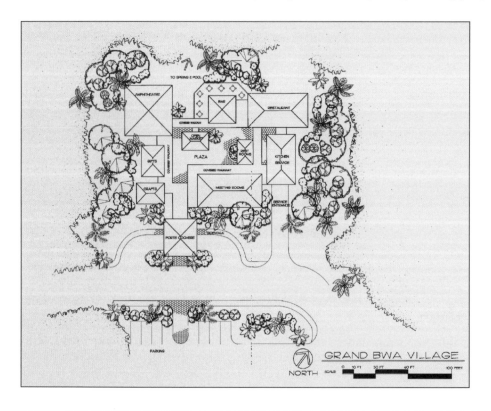

VIEW FROM VILLAGE RESTAURANT

developed area of the site along the trails and around the buildings will become a botanical garden. Currently, anthuriums are planted on several acres. Orchids, anthuriums, haliconias, tree ferns and other tropical plants will be cultivated. The gardens, when they develop to maturity, will be among the resort's most beautiful attractions.

## Resort Franchise, Management and Worldwide Reservations Systems

Grand Bwa Lodge will be flagged as a Clarion Carriage House Inn as a part of the Choice Hotels International, Worldwide Reservations Network. Clarion Carriage House Inns offer small luxury inns and hotels the opportunity to capitalize on the marketing and reservations clout of Choice Hotels International without altering their distinctive features. Clarion Carriage House Inns enjoy the benefits of belonging to the world's largest hotel franchising system, while retaining their individual imprint. Richfield Hotel Management Inc., with corporate offices in Dallas, Texas, will be the hotel operator. Richfield's extensive management training programs at Grand Bwa will train Dominicans for all levels of resort operations.

## Sustainability and the Host Land

Sustainable resort design should provide a measurable contribution to the betterment of the host island. Grand Bwa will provide the following:

- Opportunity for local ownership/investment in the resort with local partners and investors;

- hotel management training program for local staff;

- entrepreneurial opportunity for independent contract services of tour guides, craftspeople, farmers, cooks and gardeners;

- assistance to the National Park through the Adopt a Trail Program. The Grand Bwa Lodge and Wilderness Resort, as a member of the Dominica Hotel Association, proposes to establish an Adopt a Trail Program. Association members will adopt, clean and maintain portions of the National Park Trail System;

- financial assistance for the National Park. Grand Bwa will place donation cards in each guest room to provide an opportunity, for guests to add a direct voluntary cash contribution to the National Park on their hotel bill.

# Seven Spirit Bay, Northern Territory

*By Ralf Buckley*

Seven Spirit Bay (SSB) is a luxury ecotourism retreat on the shores of Coral Bay in Cobourg Peninsula, Northern Territory, Australia. Transfer time from Darwin is 45 minutes by light plane and safari wagon. SSB can house a maximum of 48 guests, in 24 open-sided hexagonal "habitats" individually secluded in the bush. An air-conditioned social hub incorporates a five-star restaurant and bar, library and 20-seat conference room. Activities include yacht cruises, wildlife safaris, bushwalking, fishing and visits to historical settlements. Walks guided by traditional Aboriginal owners are particularly popular but not always available, taking second priority to Aboriginal business.

There are naturalists on staff to take guided wildlife walks if Aboriginal walks are not available.

Under the Cobourg Peninsula Aboriginal Land and Sanctuary Act (1981), the peninsula was declared a National Park under Aboriginal ownership. The land is held by the traditional owners through a Land Trust, and the National Park is managed by the Cobourg Peninsula Sanctuary Board (CPSB). About 50 of the traditional Aboriginal owners, or more than one-third of the total, currently live within the National Park. In 1987, the CPSB sought submissions for a major tourism development in the Coral Bay area. A wide range of proposals were submitted, some from international proponents. These ranged in scale from a large international resort to transportable cabins. Generally, those proposals offering the highest economic return were also those which were largest in scale and had highest potential environmental impacts. The CPSB selected one of the smaller-scale proposals which emphasized a minimal-impact design philosophy. Design, engineering and landscape planning were all by local firms.

In addition to the requirements of the CPSB and Traditional Owners, the conceptual design for SSB was influenced strongly by a market survey. SSB could not expect to compete in price with tourist resorts in Asia, or in ease-of-access with the resorts on the eastern Queensland coast. Supply costs and waste disposal costs are very high, so SSB can be cost effective only if it aims at the top of the market.

Gurig National Park, as it is known to its Traditional Owners, has a high diversity of coastal ecosystems, including sandy beaches, dunes, mangroves, freshwater swamps, monsoon vine thickets and areas of closed forest. Large introduced mammals such as banteng, buffalo, deer and Timor ponies have been established on Cobourg Peninsula since the last century. They have caused environmental damage, notably fouling of the freshwater swamps. At the same time, however, they provide food and potential income for the Traditional Owners – and are an attraction to visitors. Effective management of these species is a major challenge for the National Park as a whole.

A site in relatively open woodland was chosen to minimize clearing, maximize sea breezes and views and provide protection from cyclone-induced storm surges. A Preliminary Environmental Report (PER) was prepared under the Environment Assessment Act (NT). The PER considered the construction schedule and its possible environmental impacts in considerable detail. It identified the following potential impacts: Bulldozer damage during beach landings, soil erosion on access tracks, introduction of weeds and exotics, disturbance to nearshore sediment processes, increased turbidity in the bay, visual impacts, potential fuel spills, potential increases in nutrients due to runoff and seepage from septic systems, potential habitat destruction from clearance and the control of waste, toxic chemicals, fire and feral animals.

Toilets and showers separate from the guest accommodations minimize impacts of seepage while retaining views from the accommodation units. Visitors accept "bathrooms in a garden" rather than in the rooms once the rationale is explained. As there are no regular direct boat services to Darwin, on-site landfill is the only realistic option for disposal of solid wastes. The site is well away from the coastline and guest areas. All buildings are of inconspicuous design, materials and color to minimize visual impacts on other users of Coral Bay. Indeed, from across the bay the units are barely detectable, even with binoculars. An on-site engineering depot housing essential plant and maintenance equipment is fully bounded and shielded from view and casual access. Firebreaks have been established along the leased boundary, with annual protective back-burning. A pressurized ring main is installed around the building in the event of an uncontrollable wildfire.

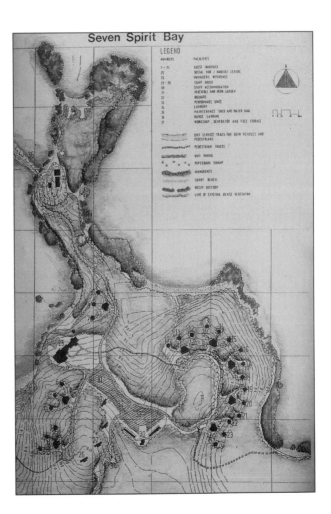

Geotextile and conveyor belt webbing were laid across the beach when the drill rig and support vehicles were brought ashore. Any vegetation cut during track clearance was laid over the foredune. Only minor earthworks were used in construction of access tracks. All service trenches were confined to access tracks. All cleared topsoil and vegetation debris was stockpiled and reused. All earth-moving equipment was cleaned before leaving Darwin, to prevent the introduction of weeds and pathogens. Plants were quarantined in a special nursery area before delivery to ensure that weeds were removed. Continuing quarantine measures are part of ongoing management. Containers for fuels, oils, paints, pesticides and other chemicals were returned to Darwin at the end of construction.

Actual impacts during construction were much as predicted. There was a marked increase in turbidity over an area several hundred metres across, but only for a short time. After initial weathering, the appearance of the barge landing is very similar to that of the surrounding cliff-face. A small beach formed quickly on the northern side of the landing, interrupting sediment drift temporarily, but drift has now resumed. The waters of the bay have long since been clear, with abundant marine life, and mangroves are colonizing the sides of the barge landing.

During construction, all staff were confined on-site by a temporary fence. All contracts included substantial penalties for access outside fenced areas, littering, damage to vegetation, importation of plants or animals, lighting fires, possessing firearms, damage to fences, contaminating soil stockpiles and interfering with the native flora and fauna.

All areas which were compacted during construction were ripped and re-graded, topsoil respread and native species replanted. Rocks and logs were replaced. The construction camp was demolished, surplus material removed to a maintenance area and protective fences removed. Irrigated amenity trees were planted around the social hub, the pool area and guest ablution units. These are weeded, pruned, fertilized and irrigated. Away from these areas, regular maintenance includes litter control, erosion control, stormwater diversion and continuing weed quarantine. All access tracks are maintained regularly.

SSB has been voted "Best Resort" at the Australian Tourism Awards as the most community and environmentally responsible resort in Australia and second only to the Hyatt On Collins (a five-star hotel in Melbourne) for quality of product and service.

With hindsight, it might have been better to build bathrooms in the rooms with sewage and sullage piped underground to a small remote treatment unit, and treated effluent used for irrigation. Initially, access was only by light plane, road, then boat; but this took so long that it became a significant market barrier, and a light aircraft strip was constructed 15 kilometers from the resort. Staff selection is difficult: Staff are screened carefully, trained and multi-skilled as far as possible.

Seven Spirit Bay started operation in April, 1990. Initial marketing was targeted very specifically at a narrow ecotourism sector, but this was not enough. Current marketing is broader. At present, about 25-30% of visitors are ecotourists in the strict sense; about 30% are there for adventure holidays in the African safari style; about 20% are there for catch-and-release fishing, at an additional charge; and about 20% visit Seven Spirit Bay principally because it has been described in upmarket travel magazines as one of the world's premier tourist destinations.

Total construction cost was $8.5 million, financed by six private shareholders. Occupancy in the first year was low, but has increased steadily since. Seven Spirit Bay has a 25-year lease on the site, with a 25-year option to extend. It pays a flat rent to the Traditional Owners, plus a proportion or turnover. The Traditional Owners have also been invited to become equity partners. There are 12 permanent staff on-site, and an additional 12 in the busy season. The average stay is about 4 days from Wednesday to Saturday; this cuts out the high-speed tourists, including most of the Japanese market. The challenge now is a financial one, to ensure that income is sufficient to cover the costs of ongoing environmental management and to provide a satisfactory return on investment.

# Coral Coast Inn, Fiji Islands –
## Ecotourism for People with Special Needs

All too often, people with special needs are excluded from full participation in the wide scope of eco-tourism experiences. Often it is the smallest detail that makes the difference between whether an event or activity is accessible or not. With careful planning and enabling attitudes, once-closed doors open to a wide and varied spectrum of experiences.

The Coral Coast Inn is on the drawing board in Fiji. It is being designed to meet the needs of people with special requirements. The architecture reflects the tropical colonial architecture of the Korotogo community – with verandas, window shutters and ceiling fans. It is designed to be compatible with the topography of the site, keeping as many of the original physical features as possible.

The site is steep; from shoreline it has a modest slope which soon gives way to a sharp rise up a ridge, with a watercourse on the western side. The advantage the slope offers is the magnificent views of the sea at all levels; the challenges are the many difficulties which must be faced by those designing for accessibility.

Ramp resting areas are designed to provide good viewing points, thus providing not only necessary pauses but also highlighting vistas at various levels of the site.

Easy access through careful design will allow freedom of movement throughout the hotel and its surrounds over three levels. The reception area, dining area, hall, lifts, meditation room, library, communal cooking area and accommodation areas are linked by covered ways that afford views of the gardens and the sea beyond.

Rooms are designed for easy accessibility with wide doors, room for turning wheelchairs and fully accessible bathrooms with appropriate grab-rails. Handles and controls in the bathrooms and on all doors as well as light switches and other electrical controls will be designed and placed for easy and safe use.

Cultural activities will be many and varied, featuring fine examples of the many cultures which make up the fabric of Fiji – indigenous Fijian (both Melanesian and Polynesian ancestry is found among indigenous Fijians), East Indian, Chinese, Micronesian, Melanesian, Polynesian and European. Traditional music as well as popular and rising local musicians will be part of the entertainment. Guests will also be invited to participate in music-making themselves or to try out musical instruments

The hall will serve not only the needs of the Coral Coast Inn, but will provide the Korotogo community with a much-needed facility. Such activities as meetings, conferences, workshops, social functions, craft fairs, musical programs, wedding receptions and a host of other activities will serve the local community as well as visitors.

A *rara* (village green), in conjunction with the hall, will provide a facility which can be used as a green area, as an entertainment area or as an extension of the hall. The flexibility offers many possibilities and will create an indoor/outdoor flow of movement and harmony.

Plant selection will include a wide variety of local fruit-bearing trees, herbal medicinal plants, perfumed and flowering plants for oil making, crafts and salusalus (traditional flower garlands). Interpretation, through guided tours, signage (Braille as well) and literature will be available.

The ecological features, historical information and traditions of this multicultural society offer vast opportunities for as simple or as varied an experience as may be desired by guests with special needs and those who provide care for them.

– Chris Saumaiwai

# Concession Planning: U.S. National Park Service

*By Robert Yearout and John Reynolds*

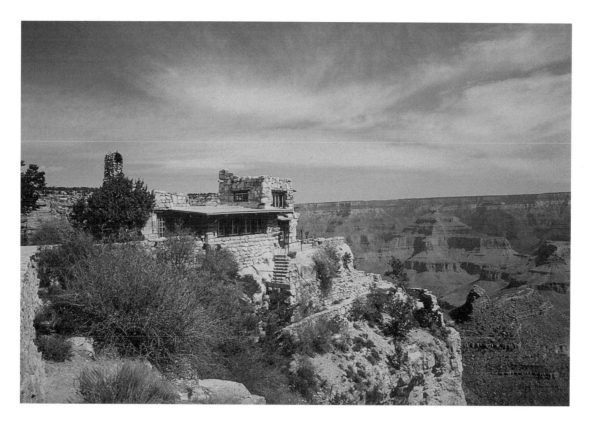

Planning for concession developments and operations at areas administered by the National Park Service (NPS) is guided by the requirements established by the U.S. Congress in its Concessions Policy Act, and policies developed to carry out the provisions of this Act. NPS policy (USNPS 1988, 10:1) reflects the intent of the Act as follows:

The National Park Service will provide, through the use of concessions, those commercial facilities and services within the parks necessary for visitors' use and enjoyment. Concession development will be limited to what is necessary and appropriate for public use and enjoyment of the parks and be consistent, to the highest degree possible, with their preservation and conservation.

In carrying out this Act, current NPS policies include a preference for out-of-park facilities provided by private enterprise instead of new or expanded development within a park, the need for planning documents to support concession development, and planning and design criteria to assure minimum impacts on park resources and values. These policies are supplemented with other guidelines on natural and cultural resources, location and site design, building design, utility considerations, maintenance and operational principles, and the interpretation of these elements of design. Sustainable design and practices have become an essential part of park planning and design, including concession facility development.

## Historical Perspective

The first parks were created in the spectacular wildlands of the West – Yosemite, Mt. Rainier, Sequoia, Yellowstone, Zion and Bryce Canyon are examples. There were no towns or villages. In many cases, there were no roads nearby. So facilities had to be built in the parks near their most important features in order for people to be able to enjoy them.

In the early part of the 20th century, even though some parks already existed, the National Park Service was born. A major effort to "bring the parks to the people" was undertaken, primarily in concert with the railroads. Spur lines were built to many parks, with lodges for guests at the end of the line. In many large parks with multiple features, roads were built, and lodges and stores built in several places in the parks. People came primarily, at first, by railroad, and rode buses around the park.

The need for people to be transported to the resource began early, because there was no other way to visit the parks in those days. Park gateway communities where people could afford to set up private service businesses did not exist, and existing communities were usually too far from the park's features.

Soon, however, the nation's growing road network came to the parks, and private automobiles came with them. As early as 1917 park superintendents were worrying about the impact of too many cars. But America's love affair with the car grew unabated, and park visitation began to expand dramatically.

It became evident in some areas that certain facilities were encroaching on park features. For example, from the very beginning, private operators were authorized to provide facilities in Yellowstone. Before the turn of the century, the Service had to remove development from Old Faithful geyser in Yellowstone because private lodges had encroached upon it.

As private cars eclipsed trains and buses as the way to see the parks, their impact on park features was magnified. Today, the impact of some "close-in" facilities and excessive automobile traffic is being recognized, and the Service is making major efforts to relocate facilities either to less sensitive areas inside parks or outside parks altogether. For example, facilities have been moved out of Yosemite Valley; all development beneath the majestic sequoias at Giant Forest in Sequoia National Park have been moved to another location; and facilities and parking have been eliminated entirely from the lake rim at Crater Lake National Park.

Many of the first lodges and service were not built to any aesthetic standard. With the advent of the railroads and their money, along with the influence of the American Society of Landscape Architects in the formation and the philosophy of the new National Park Service in 1916, the distinctive rustic architectural style of the parks was born, and to this day influences many park designs. It is a style with unique origins in the national parks and is recognized worldwide today. Its marriage of site and material is the philosophic ancestor of the sustainable design movement today.

## Concession Planning Process

The development of a NPS concession operation must be authorized by and be consistent with a park planning document which has had public input. This is usually in the form of a general management plan for the park, or a development concept plan for a specific area, both of which require formal public involvement and comment. A concession plan may then be developed to document the decision process used to determine the specifics of the concession development proposal.

A fundamental planning issue for any proposed national park concession operation is whether the facility meets the legal mandate of being "necessary and appropriate" for public use and enjoyment of a park area. A "necessary" concession operation is required in order to meet the needs of the visitor. As illustrated briefly earlier, the definition of "necessary" is changing over time. A potential concession developer should ask how guests would benefit from using the facility in terms of developing an understanding of and appreciation for the resource. An "appropriate" concession operation is compatible with the park's natural, cultural and recreational resources, and recognizes the purpose of the established area. For ecolodge development, this is also a critical concern. Changing conditions result in changing solutions.

A planning sequence is used by the Service when considering a concession development, one which would be useful to planners of ecolodge developments. These steps are considered in sequence, and failure to meet the requirements of a particular step would probably mean that the proposed service is neither necessary nor appropriate, and the process would either stop or the proposal would have to be changed.

As we go through this process, a standard set of questions is asked: 1) What is the legislative background or subsequent regulations and policy which would affect the implementation of a proposed service? 2) What park documents exist, such as general management plans or other park planning documents, which would influence implementing the proposed service? 3) What impacts or effects would this service or site have on environmental concerns, such as endangered species, floodplains or wetlands? 4) What impacts or effects would this service have upon cultural resources, such as historical preservation sites and archaeological sites? 5) What is the demand for this service? Would this service enhance the park experience? Who wants it? Is there an alternative? Is this service already being provided outside the park? Once these basic questions have been posed and answered, an economic feasibility study is done, including a market analysis, location and site analysis, refinement of the concept and a financial analysis. Failure to do this step could doom an operation to failure. Existing and future operating considerations are then considered, such as the condition of facilities, infrastructure capabilities, access, safety and sanitation issues and handicap access. During this process, the concerns of local and national interest groups and other governmental bodies and agencies are considered.

This process is particularly essential for a proposed ecolodge or national park back-country development to avoid violating the natural and human resources these developments are intended to interpret. Although this process appears to be standard procedure for development, particularly on public lands, unfortunately it is not always used.

In ecolodge development, one must also consider the effects on indigenous cultures. If the lodge tended to change those cultures, it may not be appropriate. If it tends to preserve and interpret them, it could truly become an ecolodge of great distinction.

## Design and Operational Considerations

The planning of concessions services should include design considerations that assure facilities will complement the landscape and incorporate local cultural features. However, some past design decisions have brought the city to the park or otherwise distracted from the park scene and experience. The Park Service has recently intensified its efforts in sustainable design by providing principles for park planners and designers so they could correct previous design problems as well as design new facilities which add to the park experience.

A critical element of sustainable design is its interpretive role, as illustrated by the following quote from the Service's "Guiding Principles of Sustainable Design" (USNPS 1993, 9):

> Sustainable park and ecotourism development, to be truly successful, needs to anticipate and manage human experiences. Interpretation provides the best single tool for shaping experiences and sharing values. By providing an awareness of the environment, values are taught that are necessary for the protection of the environment. Sustainable design should seek to affect not only immediate behaviors but also the long-term beliefs and attitudes of visitors.

Stephen Mather, the first Director of the National Park Service, observed during the early years of concession operations at Yellowstone: "Scenery is a hollow enjoyment to a tourist who sets out in the morning after an indigestible breakfast and a fitful sleep on an impossible bed" (Everhart 1972, 112). During the last two decades, efforts have been intensified to assure a satisfactory level of basic concession services for park visitors. Today, these efforts continue, but with additional emphasis on sustainable practices and interpretation of the park's resources.

There is more to park concession or ecolodge operations than simply providing a room, a meal, or an entertaining activity. A lodging room should instead enhance the park experience through design, materials and art. Food service should also add to the experience; as well as being of high value, it should also feature traditional menu items typical of that region.

Souvenirs and gifts should interpret the experience and feature natural and cultural themes of that park and surrounding area. Activities provided by a concessioner or ecolodge operator should be designed to allow the visitor to gain an appreciation of the resource.

Park Service management and development plans, and concession planning and contracting documents, are increasingly identifying environmental and interpretive concessioner requirements. Concessioners on their own initiative are increasing their efforts to provide their guests, and park visitors in general, an improved park experience through an understanding and appreciation of the park's resources. These efforts include environmental and sustainable operation practices, which are explained to guests. For example, Signal Mountain Lodge at Grand Teton National Park converted to natural non-toxic cleaning materials, and table-cards placed in rooms inform their guests that "We have cleaned your room and all linens with biodegradable, non-toxic, animal cruelty-free and environmentally safe products." They go on to say that "We have a recycling program. Please, leave glass, aluminum, newspapers and magazines in your room." Guests are also told that although

they may have clean towels every day by placing them in the tub after use, it would be preferable to hang the towels on racks to reduce the use of water and power. Most guests hang up the towels. These efforts are important to the Service; by virtue of where they operate, national park concessioners should be leaders in providing the types of experiences one would expect from a sustainable ecolodge operation.

These experiences vary from front-country concessions operations, such as in Yosemite Valley or Mesa Verde National Park, to back-country operation, such as Brooks Camp in Katmai National Park or the Glacier National Park chalets. In either situation, the concessioner's operation should have a positive effect on the interpretation of as well as minimal impact on the park's fragile natural and cultural resources.

A case in point is the proposed plan for Brooks Camp, which features brown bear viewing, fishing, archaeological interpretation, and trips to a volcanic area, the Valley of Ten Thousand Smokes. The primary access to this small concession facility and NPS campground is by floatplane, with some visitors arriving by boat. The lodge, cabins and both concessioner and NPS employee and maintenance facilities are located on what is now generally accepted as an exceptionally important archaeological site which is also a travel corridor for bears. Visitation to Brooks Camp has increased measurably in the last few years, primarily by day-use visitors. The proposed plan calls for moving lodging, campground and other facilities across the Brooks River to an area not frequented much by the bears, and with far fewer and more dispersed archaeological sites. Visitation limits would be controlled, and interpretive tours and shuttles to bear-viewing areas, archaeological sites and the volcanic area would be improved. Facilities would then be removed from the existing developed area, which would be closed to human use, except for occasional archaeological work.

There are similar lodges throughout the world which have developed over a period of time when an understanding of natural and cultural impacts has also evolved. Other developments in fragile or pristine areas have been planned, constructed and continue to operate without adequate appreciation of their effects on the resources. Careful and complete planning efforts are critical steps to take by both governmental agencies, local and national, and private sector developers to assure that development and management of such facilities are accomplished in a manner sensitive to these resources.

The National Park Service and its concessioners can learn from the successes and failures of ecolodge developments around the world. The world can also benefit from the efforts made in national parks.

### Literature cited:

Everhart, William C. 1972. "The National Park Service." Prager Publishers, New York.

USNP5 (U.S. National Park Service). 1988. "Management Policies, U.S. National Park Service." USNPS Denver Service Center, Denver.

USNPS. 1993. "Guiding Principles of Sustainable Design." USNPS Denver Service Center, Denver.

# Afterword

By Cynthia A. Grippaldi

Ecotourism is to a large extent driven by consumer demands from distant locations. The marketing and the emphasis is on the end product as experienced by the tourist. This is leading to a situation of tourism taking priority over the ecological uniqueness of an area to the point at which the tourism 'cart' is in some places leaving the 'eco-horse' in the dust. This creates a momentum which is difficult to control. At a recent ecotourism management seminar, for example, the Deputy Director of the Department of Tourism in Nepal made a startling statement. After years of adventure travelers/ecotravelers visiting the environmental attractions in his country and leaving ecological and cultural pollution in their wake, he posed the question: "Is ecotourism nothing more than tourism in ecologically sensitive areas?"

For ecotourism to be sustainable, it is essential to bridge generations and train youth as qualified replacements for today's stewards. Communities must foster local constituents who will be supporters of natural resources and see them as more than just a way to make money. Too often, locals are required to forego the use of resources in order to protect them for the visiting public at large. This can lead to a resentment of and lack of value and appreciation for a resource. Without the vital connection of education there is no learned appreciation to support the ecologically sound management of protected areas.

As an example, many of the local Virgin Islands youth are at best uncomfortable with, at worst afraid of, the ocean. Most of these fears have been passed down through the generations and, as a result, an important link with marine conservation is neglected. At the Virgin Islands Environmental Resource Station, a program I manage, Eco-camp offers snorkeling lessons to local youngsters. It is an amazing experience to provide these children with the equipment, education and supervision they need to feel safe enough to enter the ocean and see it for the first time. They immediately become fascinated with the underwater world, venture farther than they ever dared before, and are reluctant to get out of the water! If they are to be our future resource managers, they must have positive experiences early in life with all of their environments.

There is no substitute for the proper planning of long-term, ecologically sound management of protected areas. I do not use the term Sustainable

Development because it has the potential to be an oxymoron as it stands. Development can sustain many things, few of which are environmentally advantageous. Sustainable Development often joins the ranks of buzzwords used to 'green wash' development projects into appearing more environmentally correct.

Ecolodges alone cannot provide true ecotourism. The responsibilities that accompany the designation are far-reaching throughout the environmental and social communities and are not confined to a place to sleep. Many of the problems now faced in protected areas throughout the world are a result of private sector tourism activities which have moved ahead at a rate that far outdistances the capacity of the area or park to manage. We can not afford to allow our environmental resources to be reduced to playgrounds. Economic benefits from tourism endeavors must be channeled back into integrated resource management through training, conservation and research programs, infrastructure upgrades, visitor management and adequate protection enforcement. Implied or trickle-down conservation and education is not enough. For ecotourism to succeed, it must be holistic and embrace all environmental and social concerns through proper planning and limits based on carrying capacities and education.

# Resources

# Pacific Yurts

*By Alan Bair*
*Pacific Yurts Inc.*

## Connecting Ancient Wisdom with Modern Technology

Inspired by the practicality of the traditional yurts of Mongolian nomads, we have developed a lightweight, low-cost version that retains the sense of wholeness of the ancient form while delivering the quality of light and structural integrity demanded by modern users. Typically set upon decks supported by simple post and beam systems, the Pacific Yurts have a minimum impact on the surrounding soils and, though durable, can be removed without a trace if necessary. Complete kits weigh only a few hundred pounds, and since their design in 1978 they have been shipped all over the world. They have been erected as recreational structures in public parks and commercial resorts and used widely by private individuals. Their flexibility allows them to work both as simple cabins and fully furnished luxury retreats in ski country and in tropical settings. Key players in the ecotourism movement, these award-winning yurts are nondestructive to delicate ecosystems and adaptable to a variety of conventional and alternative energy and water/waste technologies.

## Design and Construction

Our yurts are framed in wood and sheathed in custom-formulated thermoplastic architectural fabrics. The walls are made of a continuous lattice of kiln-dried Douglas fir lath. The lattice is bolted to the deck and it supports an aircraft-quality tension cable. Supported by the cable are radial 2x3 or 2x4 rafters with steel pins that insert into a laminated fir compression ring at the top, which is covered by an acrylic dome skylight. The vinyl top cover is laced to the wall with nylon cord and an overlapping valance to ensure a weathertight fit. Standard features include a lockable door and two windows covered with 20-mil clear vinyl, with a French door and additional windows available as options. All the wood is finished with a clear penetrating oil finish, and all the standard components are made in Oregon either from farmed, second-growth wood or from material that can later be recycled. The top cover has up to a 15-year warranty, comparable to the roofs of more permanent structures.

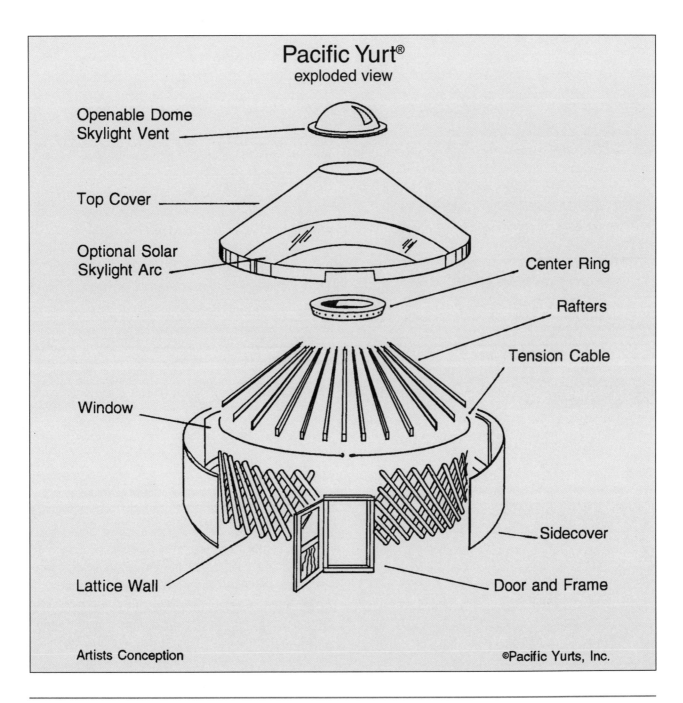

**Pacific Yurt®**
exploded view

Openable Dome Skylight Vent

Top Cover

Optional Solar Skylight Arc

Center Ring

Rafters

Tension Cable

Window

Sidecover

Lattice Wall

Door and Frame

Artists Conception

©Pacific Yurts, Inc.

Other options include entrance awnings, a translucent arc integrated into the top cover for additional daylighting, 2x3 studs under each rafter engineered to support snow loads, NASA-developed reflective insulation, water catchment systems and heaters. Unlike other recreational structures, these yurts can accommodate the handicapped with wider doors, levers for door handles and sloped ramps on the access thresholds.

The compact shape of the yurt and the combination of lightweight members in tension and compression mean that the structure is highly efficient in maximizing strength while minimizing material. The efficiency of material also means that the yurt kits are relatively inexpensive to ship. They fit comfortably in the back of a small pickup truck and they are easy for two people to assemble. The yurt kits vary from a weight of 700 pounds, including shipping crate, for the 12-foot diameter version, to 2200 pounds for the 30-foot one. Four other intermediate sizes are also available.

Our basic yurt kit does not include the supporting deck, although instructions and a materials list for building decks are included. This means that the deck materials can be bought locally and more economically. We recommend post and beam construction supported by concrete piers, but slabs on grade or rammed earth are also feasible. Once the deck is built, the customer can assemble the yurt in less than a day.

## A Fit with Ecotourism

A variety of characteristics has made the yurt particularly appropriate for ecotourism. A choice of wall and roof colors enable each yurt to adapt to its local environment. Its organic shape helps it blend into its surroundings. The post and beam-supported deck means a low impact on the earth below.

The broad range of options gives the yurts added flexibility. The insulation, heater and rafter supports make them ideal for ski country, while a tinted, openable dome, reflective roof insulation and additional screened windows for ventilation make them comfortable in the tropics. In installations from Australia to Saudi Arabia, from Hawaii to Alaska, these yurts have provided thermal comfort to adventurers and vacationers. The basic kit yields a Spartan back-country shelter, while equipping them with energy, water and waste

handling systems gives inhabitants all the comforts of home. And the range of sizes makes the yurt appropriate for anything from a small studio to a spacious meeting hall. They have been approved by the U.S. Forest Service and are in use by the Oregon State Parks Department and commercial resorts worldwide.

Though generally classified as "tents," yurts are stronger and more weathertight than conventional tents. Because they can be erected in remote locations, they give inhabitants the opportunity to feel a connection to nature and at the same time experience comfort, security and protection from even harsh environments.

## Adaptations and Applications

Another key to the yurts' adaptability is the flexibility of their circular floor plans. Some users build interior partitions and even sleeping lofts in the larger sizes. Extended decks and covered walkways connecting multiple yurts create multi-room dwellings. Windows can be located to face scenic views in any direction.

Because the walls and floor can be penetrated anywhere, the yurts can accommodate virtually any conventional plumbing, electrical or heating system. But because they tend to be installed in remote locations, it's equally likely that alternative systems are chosen. These could include propane stoves, photovoltaic cell-powered refrigerators, composting toilets and so on. Unlike other recreational structures designed for ecotourism, no particular systems are imposed on users by the manufacturer.

And because the yurts can accommodate a variety of options, from the minimal to the luxurious, they make a good fit with more permanent structures. For example, a resort might have a central lodge or large yurt with all the amenities and offer basic yurts as satellite cabins. In some cases, such as on ecologically delicate parkland, this strategy might enable resort planners to extend their "development" onto otherwise unbuildable land.

Indeed, this technology may prove to be a practical solution in the ongoing debate between those who want to develop the resorts and those who want to protect nature. Yurts may be the key because they enable developers to create a profitable infrastructure, offer vacationers access to the natural environment and assure conservationists of a minimum impact on the earth.

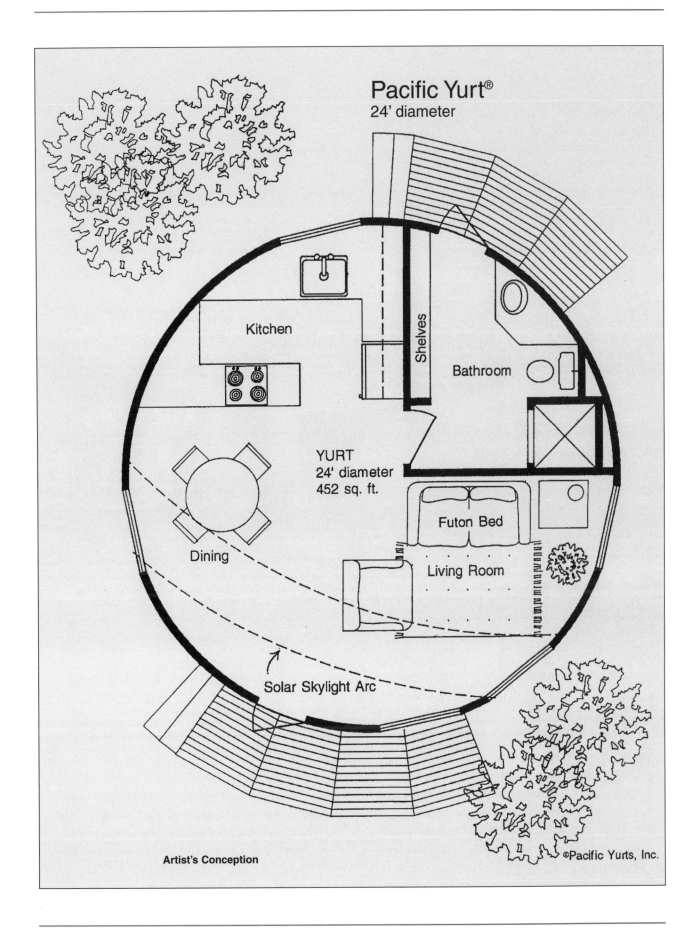

# Pacific Yurt®
## 24' diameter

Kitchen

Shelves

Bathroom

YURT
24' diameter
452 sq. ft.

Dining

Futon Bed

Living Room

Solar Skylight Arc

**Artist's Conception**

©Pacific Yurts, Inc.

# Ecotents

*By James Hadley and Joe Hardesty*
*Maho Bay Camps*

The new tents being planned for Estate Concordia on the southeast shore of St. John in the Virgin Islands are a further development of an idea that began on St. John in 1974. As a building type, these canvas cottages have been in almost continual evolution since the inception of Maho Bay Camps, with the ecotents being the most recent step. A short history of this evolution will provide a background:

1. The earliest Maho Bay tents were designed to be prefabricated entirely in the United States and hung from a wooden support structure built on site in the Virgin Islands. They were based on a 16x16-foot platform divided into four 8x8-foot segments for living, kitchen/dining, sleeping and outdoor deck. All initial cottages were of this type and a number of them remained until the 1980s.

Although they were easily assembled after building the frame, they required patching when portions were damaged or were discarded as a unit if damage was excessive.

All tent cottages included kitchens with camping-type stoves and minimal electricity from the Virgin Islands power grid. Running water and toilets were remote from the cottages in common bath houses.

2. As a result of the patching process, it was discovered that the tents could be prefabricated in sections, and sections replaced when damaged. This change resulted in the canvas being positioned over the frame and nailed or stapled to it, rather than being slung below the frame.

3. The continued replacement of rolling window flaps and zippered (later velcro) door flaps encouraged Maho Bay staff to replace these items with ventilator slots and screen doors. By this time, the tents had become fabric-covered frame structures of a unique relationship to the Virgin Islands climate. They were being built with fabrics with enhanced life spans that had been created during the years of the resort's growth. They still lacked plumbing, however.

4. The final section of Maho Bay tents was built with a wind scoop utilizing the venturi effect of the roof shape and orientation to the prevailing breezes to provide passive ventilation for the structures.

5. The construction of Harmony, a luxury resort with buildings unconnected to the island's power grid, suggested that tent cottages could also be supplied with amenities without need for an infrastructure. This led to the "ecotent."

The ecotents are therefore the beneficiaries of twenty years of testing and growth of a building system that is unique to Maho Bay. They provide a loft space as an addition to the basic Maho Bay tent described above. They also provide at every cottage:

- Prefabricated water storage tanks (cisterns) under the floors;
- composting toilets and a solar-heated shower;
- a photovoltaic array for power generation and batteries for storage of electricity;
- refrigerator (either electric or gas).

They represent a completely new building type for semitropical areas. Three different designs for the tents are being built and will be studied to assess the relative virtues of the various plan modifications.

Future models may include adaptations in response to problems or guest comments. Primary concerns as part of the ongoing research will include

*First Maho tent – slung under frame*

GUTTERS ON TENTS COLLECT RAINWATER

WALKS MEANDER THRU VEGETATION

VEGETATION SCREENS COTTAGES

WALKS ABOVE GRADE DISTRIBUTE PEOPLE, UTILITIES

COTTAGES RAISED ABOVE THE GROUND FOR VIEWS, MINIMUM DISTURBANCE OF VEGETATION & WILDLIFE

*Typical early tent layout*

*Second type of tent with panelized construction*

wind resistance, ventilation, water collection, energy use, materials performance, safety and livability. Elements such as efficient storage, sleeping spaces and general daytime uses for dining, cooking, etc. will be evaluated. New and old technologies will be compared. The result is education.

In addition, inventory of existing vegetation as it relates to slope, aspect and elevation will be done by using transects across the site. The effects of the new construction and of using gray water for irrigation can be monitored and evaluated over time against this baseline data.

# The Geo-Lite™ Ecolodge

*By Bob Galbreath*
*Geo-Lite Systems*

## A New Approach to Resort Lodging: The Geo-Lite Ecolodge

Geo-Lite Systems is a new joint venture by two California corporations (Garden Technology, Inc. and KenCom, Inc.) formed to market, install and service a new type of modular dwelling. While this dwelling has a number of promising uses, we designed it specifically with ecotourism in mind.

Geo-Lite Systems is primarily a construction company with a single very specialized product. The major experience of the joint venture companies is in installation of technical hardware in remote sites with a "minor" in the construction of buildings to house that hardware. We have worked in the Bahamas and the Aleutians and many stops in between. The quality and ecological sensitivity of the lodgings available to us in

many of these locations has been minimal. We decided we could do better and the Geo-Lite unit was our first offering.

A Geo-Lite prototype unit began operation in California in late 1994.

## The System

The Geo-Lite unit is a self-sufficient dwelling system that requires no connections to utility services. Each unit is calibrated to a certain range of occupancy (2 to 4 persons, 4 to 6, 8 to 10). Each unit generates its own electricity, recycles its own waste and stores and pumps its own water. (An external water source is required.)

The dwelling is composed of one or more bedroom areas, separated from the living area by folding screens, and a bathroom containing a lavatory, shower and flush toilet. Efficiency kitchens are available in larger units.

The dwelling sits on a modular platform supported by small-diameter columns. The raised platform conceals all of the support equipment except the solar panels. The platform may be varied in size to accommodate outdoor amenities such as picnic tables and recreation equipment.

## Ecolodge Features

The Geo-Lite unit was specifically designed for minimum ecological impact. Its environmentally-sensitive features include:

• *clean power/clean waste* – solar power (wind or hydro also, if appropriate), composting toilets and gray water systems reduce resource consumption. The need for utility infrastructure and hazardous waste disposal is eliminated;

• *adaptability to local cultural styles* – two of the dwellings offered for the Geo-Lite unit are cylindrical structures with conical roofs. The third is somewhat Victorian in appearance. Exterior surface materials can be varied in all three styles. This feature, plus

the location of the dwelling on a raised platform, results in a structure which blends with many of the architectural styles found in undeveloped regions;

• *tangible eco-experiences* – for participation-oriented resorts, the Geo-Lite unit can be configured with energy and waste systems more accessible to the guests, providing, if desired, a "live-in science lab" atmosphere. Optional equipment allows guests to electronically monitor their own energy use and waste recycling.

## Unique Geo-Lite Features

While many of the features described above are found at other ecotourism resorts, the Geo-Lite unit is unique in several notable aspects:

• *variety of applications* – the flexibility of the Geo-Lite system allows it to be tailored to a wide variety of climate variations, site conditions, comfort levels and numbers of occupants. While conceived with ecologically sensitive recreation in mind, the Geo-Lite system offers a much wider range of comfort options than traditional forms of remote-area shelter. The units are unusually spacious, ranging in size from 340 to over 700 square feet (32 to 65 square meters)

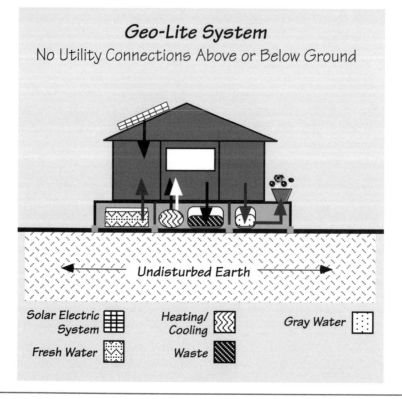

with ceiling heights up to 14 feet (4.25 meters). If desired, features not normally associated with adventure travel such as carpeting, fireplaces, stereo and microwave ovens can be accommodated;

- *worldwide transportability* – whichever configuration is chosen, the entire system can be transported in a standard overseas shipping container.

- *a very small footprint* – no grading is necessary. The unit rests on small diameter, non-continuous footings requiring little, if any, excavation;

- *non-consumptive construction methods* – The entire unit is constructed of recycled and/or recyclable materials with removable fasteners and can be completely disassembled and reused without waste;

- *relocatable* – as a result of the features described above, the unit can be moved to another site with little evidence of its past presence, permitting natural habitat regeneration without loss of lodging income. However, the unit's modular nature does not prevent it from being left in place and, when assembled, it does not look temporary;

- *truly sustainable design* – the modular, relocatable, reusable nature of Geo-Lite units allows a feature that we believe is unique in the resort industry: leasing of lodging units – the ultimate in "cradle-to-grave" responsibility. Geo-Lite Systems is developing a lease system for units constructed in groups of three or more.

# Design Points for People with Handicaps

*Chris Saumaiwai*
*Principal, Coral Coast Inn, Suva, Fiji*

Ecolodge developers focus on the special needs of our environment and how we can not only be in harmony with those needs but also experience its uniqueness.

This presentation focuses on PEOPLE with special needs and on ways to plan or adapt not only to accommodate their special needs but also to ensure an environment for a full and varied experience.

## Considerations in Meeting Special Needs of People Who are:

### Physically Handicapped

1. **Wheelchair dependent**
   - Ramps/slopes/paths - to recognized standards
   - Pausing stops/passing areas
   - Entryways easily accessible
   - Turning circles
   - Floor surfaces - appropriate for good mobility, but not slippery, even when wet
   - Accessible toilets
   - Appropriate lifts/elevators
   - Appropriate tables/counters, etc. at convenient levels
   - Appropriate bathrooms
   - Displays at appropriate heights
   - Handles/controls/power points/switches at appropriate heights

2. **Crutch/cane/walker/etc. dependent**
   In addition to any applicable items previously listed:
   - Handrails – discreet, not to look institutional
   - Floor surfaces – not slippery, even when wet

3. **Stroke patients**
   In addition to any applicable items previously listed:
   - The effects of a stroke may include perceptual problems as well as physical problems

- Avoid mosaic patterns on floors or sharply contrasting linoleum squares (the dark and light squares may be perceived to be at different heights)

### Visually Handicapped

1. **Totally blind**
   - Make sure hazards such as edges of ramps, swimming pools, etc. have rails, raised curbs or other appropriate indications to prevent accidents
   - Menus/activity lists/information sheets should be provided in Braille (or audio tape where appropriate)

2. **Sight impaired**
   - Adequate lighting must be provided – particularly on paths, ramps and passages
   - Menus/activity lists/etc. must be in large, clear print and easy to read
   - Clearly mark changing floor levels – ramps, slopes, steps, etc.

3. **Problems with glare**
   - Carefully plan lighting to avoid glare
   - Know where to seat people to avoid glare where required

### Hearing Impaired

1. **Totally Hearing Impaired and Speech Impaired**
   - Availability of staff totally conversant with sign language
   - Light signals in substitution for audio – telephone communication devices, door knocker, etc.

2. **Partially Deaf**
   - Staff training in assisting partially deaf

# Resource Organizations

*By Susan Buse*

## I. Ecotourism:

The following organizations serve as sources of information on the environmental and cultural impacts of tourism; the expanding ecotourism industry; planning, management, and development for ecotourism and other topics. Publications, reports, and other resources are listed after the organization's name and contact information. These materials are excellent resources for further study.

**Conservation International, 1015 18th St. NW, Washington, DC 20036 USA. Phone: 202-887-5188.**

*Ecotourism: The Uneasy Alliance.* 1989. A thorough investigation into the market for ecotourism, detailing the structure of the nature tourism industry and its potential for success as a local economic development tool. Distributed by the Ecotourism Society, 802-447-2121 (see below).

**The Ecotourism Society, POBox 755, North Bennington, VT 05257 U.S.A. Phone: 802-447-2121, Fax: 802-447-2122.**

(1) *Ecotourism: A Guide for Planners and Managers,* 1993. A practical guide to the basic elements of successful ecotourism projects and how to implement ecotourism principles in the field, offering case studies and examples from around the world. (2) *Ecotourism Guidelines for Nature Tour Operators,* 1993. Provides up-to-date standards for the operation of tours in fragile natural areas. Useful for professionals throughout the travel industry. (3) *The Ecotourism Society Newsletter.* Quarterly international news covering current issues, listings of relevant events, and the latest ecotourism publications. (4) *The Ecotourism Society Annotated Bibliography.* A fully annotated bibliography that focuses on ecotourism as it pertains to international conservation, economic development, sustainable design and other related areas.

**International Institute of Tourism Studies, The George Washington University, School of Business and Public Management, 817 23rd St. NW, Washington, DC 20052 USA. Phone: 202-994-6281, Fax: 202-994-1420.**

(1) *The Tourism and Environment Partnership: Putting the Pieces Together.* A video plus an accompanying Video Workbook Supplement addressing the relationship between sustainable and environmentally-oriented tourism and conservation of the natural environment. (2) *Tourism, Health, and the Environment: Prescription for a Partnership.* A video documentary which explores the relationship of tourism to health and environmental issues, and the growing demand for health motivated travel. (3) *Global Assessment of Tourism Policy.* A video and written report presenting the major issues to be addressed by tourism policy-makers over the next decade.

**National Audubon Society, 700 Broadway, New York, NY 10003 USA. Phone: 212-979-3000, Fax: 212-979-3188.**

*Travel Ethic for Environmentally Responsible Travel.* Comprehensive guidelines dealing with consideration for wildlife, industry waste disposal, supporting conservation efforts, and respect for other cultures. The guidelines were originally established for the organization's tour operators and travel companies.

**National Ocean and Atmospheric Administration (NOAA), U.S. Department of Commerce, 1825 Connecticut Ave. NW, Washington, DC 20235 USA. Phone: 202-606-4436, Fax: 202-606-4057.**

*U.S. Federal Agency Assistance for Ecotourism Activities,* 1993. A handbook of U.S. federal agencies with information on tourism activities within marine and coastal areas. Intended to help guide inquirers directly to the sources of U.S. government information.

*North American Coordinating Center for Responsible Tourism, POBox 827, San Anselmo, CA 94979 USA. Phone: 415-258-6594, Fax: 415-454-2493.*

Publishes a quarterly newsletter and serves as an information clearinghouse on responsible travel.

*United Nations Environment Programme (UNEP), Room DC2-0803, United Nations Plaza, New York, NY 10017 USA. Phone: 212-963-8139.*

*UNEP Industry and Environment*, Vol 15, No. 3–4, July–December 1992. A special journal issue devoted to sustainable tourism development and ecotourism.

*United States Travel and Tourism Administration (USTTA), Office of Research, U.S. Department of Commerce, HCHB Room 1868, 14th and Constitution Ave. NW, Washington, DC 20230 USA. Phone: 202-482-4028, Fax: 202-482-2887.*

USTTA's Office of Research provides tourism statistics on U.S. travelers going overseas, and overseas travelers coming to the U.S.

*World Tourism Organization (WTO), Capitan Haya, 42, 28020 Madrid, Spain. Phone: 34 (1) 571-06-28, Fax: 34(1)571-37-33.*

(1) *Guidelines: Development of National Parks and Protected Areas for Tourism*, 1992. This guide discusses park development and management plans, staffing and marketing of protected area sites for tourism, and provides descriptions of park tourism development projects. (2) *Sustainable Tourism Development: Guide for Local Planners*, 1993. A practical handbook for local policy makers and planners on planning for sustainable tourism development.

*World Travel and Tourism Environment Research Center (WTTERC), OCTALS, Oxford Brookes University, Gipsy Lane, Headington, Oxford, UK 0X3 OPB. Phone: 44-865-819-908, Fax: 44-865-819-907.*

*World Travel & Tourism Environment Review*, 1993. This review discusses key travel and tourism industry environmental issues, summarizes industry efforts to improve environmental performance, and indicates future progress the industry must make in order to achieve environmentally compatible growth.

*World Wildlife Fund (WWF), 1250 24th St. NW, Washington, DC 20037 USA. Phone: 202-293-4800.*

(1) *Ecotourism: The Potentials and Pitfalls, Volume 1 and 2*, 1990. Volume I examines nature tourism, its impacts, and its links to conservation and protected natural areas. Volume 2 evaluates ecotourism's impacts in five developing countries. Distributed by the Ecotourism Society. (2) *The Ecotourism Boom: Planning for Development and Management*, 1992. A diagnostic and set of planning guidelines for development and management of ecotourism to be used in the creation of ecotourism strategies for protected natural areas and local communities. (3) *An Analysis of Ecotourism's Economic Contribution to Conservation and Development in Belize*, Volume 1 and 2, 1994. A report on research undertaken to address the impacts of ecotourism in Belize, which includes background information and recommendations for further increasing tourism's contribution to conservation and local and national economies. Volume I is a Summary Report, Volume 2 is the Comprehensive Report. Distributed by the Ecotourism Society.

## II. Sustainable Design and Renewable Energy:

These organizations serve as sources of information on sustainable design and development. Information on using environmentally sensitive landscaping, architecture, and building technologies; renewable energy sources; recycled building materials and other strategies related to sustainability. Publications, reports, and other resources are listed after the organization's name and contact information. These materials are useful for further study. An additional list of recommended reading resources has also been provided.

*American Institute of Architects (AIA), Committee on the Environment (COTE), 735 New York Ave. NW, Washington, DC 20006 USA. Phone: 202-626-7300.*

*Environmental Resource Guide*. The quarterly COTE publication addresses critical issues, discusses case studies, and offers bibliographic resources and contacts on the topics of site design and land use, natural resources, energy, recycling and waste management and building ecology.

*American Society of Landscape Architects (ASLA), 4401 Connecticut Ave. NW, 5th floor, Washington, DC 20008 USA. Phone: 202-686-2752.*

(1) *Landscape Architecture*, Volume 82, No. 81, August 1992. A special issue of the journal of the ASLA devoted to landscape architecture's role in ecotourism and sustainable development, with articles describing projects in Bali, Cyprus, Belize, India, the U.S. Virgin Islands, and Taiwan. (2) *Landscape Architecture*, Volume 84, No. 1, January 1994. A special issue highlighting the increasingly active involvement of landscape architects in exploring and implementing new approaches to sustainable design.

*Center for Resourceful Building Technology, POBox 3866, Missoula, MT 59806 USA. Phone: 406-549-7678, Fax: 406-549-4100.*

*Guide to Resource Efficient Building Elements (GREBE), 4th Edition.* Provides developers, builders, architects, and consumers with a reference to suppliers of alternative and recycled building products, including contact information for companies, descriptions of products and discussions of resource efficiency. Updated yearly.

*Environmental Building News, R.R. 1, Box 161, Brattleboro, VT 05301 USA. Phone: 802-257-7300, Fax: 802-257-7304.*

(1) *Environmental Building News.* A bimonthly newsletter on environmentally sustainable design and construction which regularly publishes lists of manufacturers of "green" building products. (2) *Annotated Bibliography*, 1993. A comprehensive bibliography of the best publications available on green building technology.

*Green Builder Program, City of Austin, Environmental and Conservation Services Department., 206 E. 9th Street, Suite 17.102, Austin, TX 78701 USA. Phone: 512-499-3500, Fax: 512-499-2859.*

*Sustainable Building Sourcebook*, 1993. A reference book providing definitions, design considerations, and implementation issues relating to sustainable building, including sections on water, energy, building materials, and solid waste applications. Oriented to a southwestern climate but still useful for its wealth of information.

*Green Building Council, 1615 L St. NW, Suite 1200, Washington, DC 20036 USA. Phone: 1-800-727-7070.*

(1) *Green Building Conference*, 1994. NIST Special Publication 863. Proceedings of a conference co-sponsored by the U.S Green Building Council and the National Institute of Standards and Technology (NIST). Contains papers presented by speakers on topics such as performance assessment criteria for green buildings, product life cycle assessment, the future of green building technology, and case studies of green building programs. (2) *Local Government Sustainable Buildings Guidebook: Environmentally Responsible Building Design and Management*, March 1994. Provides an introduction and overview of sustainable construction and renovation strategies, from the predesign to demolition phases. Distributed by Public Technology, Inc. Phone: 800-852-4934, or 202-626-2412.

*Interior Concerns, POBox 2386, Mill Valley, CA 94942 USA. Phone: 415-389-8049, Fax: 415-388-8322.*

(1) *Interior Concerns Resource Guide: A Guide to Sustainable and Healthy Products and Educational Information for Designing and Building*, 1993. Offers current educational information, listings of environmentally sensitive products and manufacturers, case studies of existing eco-buildings, consultants, and listings of additional ecological and sustainable design oriented resources for further research. (2) *Interior Concerns Newsletter:* A bimonthly newsletter for environmentally concerned designers, architects, and building professionals.

*Maho Bay Camps, Inc. and Harmony Resort, 17A East 73rd St., New York City, NY 10021-3578 USA. Phone: 1-800-392-9004 or 212-472-9453, Fax: 212-861-6210.*

(1) *Harmony: A Sustainable Development Research-Resort – Building Materials Source Book.* A complete guide to the building materials used in construction of Harmony Resort, a state-of-the-art resort constructed entirely of recycled materials and which operates on solar and wind power.

**National Park Service (NPS), United States Department of the Interior, Denver Service Center, 12795 W. Alameda Parkway, POBox 25287, Denver, CO 80225-0287 USA. Phone: 303-969-2130.**

(1) *Environmentally Responsible Building Product Guide*, 1992. Provides information about the "cradle-to-grave" effects of various building materials, and suggests appropriate choices of materials, as well as other concerns to consider when selecting building products. (2) *Guiding Principles of Sustainable Design*, 1993. A comprehensive manual for planners, architects, and developers which presents sustainability principles for integrating natural and cultural resource conservation into the development of sites for tourism.

**Rocky Mountain Institute, Green Development Services Program, 1739 Snowmass Creek Road, Snowmass, CO 81654 USA. Phone: 303-927-3851, Fax: 303-927-4178.**

(1) *Graywater Systems, Composting Toilets, and Rainwater Collection Systems: A Resource List*. A guide to relevant books, articles, manufacturers and organizations that deal with water conserving systems. (2) *Rocky Mountain Institute Newsletter*. The semi-annual newsletter reporting on community energy planning, water conservation, sustainable agriculture, economic renewal and other issues dealing with efficient and sustainable use of resources.

**The Society for Ecological Restoration (SER), 1207 Seminole Hwy., Madison, WI 53711 USA. Phone/Fax: 608-262-9547.**

(1) *Restoration Ecology*. A quarterly scientific journal of restoration theory and technical articles. (2) *Restoration & Management Notes*. A semi-annual summary of ecological restoration techniques, technical advances in restoration, and restoration projects. (3) *SER News*. The quarterly newsletter, including articles on restoration activities.

## III. Renewable Energy Technologies:

The following U.S. government agencies and trade associations are involved in research, technical assistance, and distribution of publications, reports, and other resources on renewable energy technology including solar energy, wind energy, biofuels, recycling, etc. Publications are listed after the organization's name and contact information.

### U.S. Department of Energy

**Energy Efficiency and Renewable Energy Clearinghouse (EREC), POBox 3048, Merrifield, VA 22116 USA. Phone: 800-363-3732, Fax: 1-703-893-0400.**

*Fact sheets* are provided by EREC on a wide range of energy topics including passive solar design, energy efficient appliances, biofuels production, small-scale hydro, recycling and others.

**National Renewable Energy Laboratory (NREL), Technical Inquiry Service,1617 Cole Blvd., Golden, CO 80401 USA. Phone: 303-275-4099, Fax: 303-275-4091.**

(1) *General interest publications*. Nontechnical publications are available from NREL which cover a wide variety of energy efficiency and conservation subjects. (2) *NREL Technical Reports*. Provides technical information on energy research and analysis projects, targeted at knowledgeable technical professionals.

**Sandia National Laboratories, Renewable Energy Design Assistance Center, Mail Stop 0704, POBox 5800, Albuquerque, NM 87185-0704 USA. Phone: 505-844-7594, Fax: 505-844-7786.**

Sandia National Laboratories has an extensive array of publications, information, and materials available through its Solar Thermal Design Assistance Center, its Renewable Energy Office, and its Photovoltaic Design Assistance Center. For listings of these publications contact Sandia National Laboratories.

### Trade Associations

**American Wind Energy Association (AWEA), 122 C St. NW, 4th floor, Washington, DC 20001 USA. Phone: 202-383-2500, Fax: 202-383-2505.**

(1) *Wind Energy for Sustainable Development*, 1992. Describes the variety of wind technology applications for fulfilling energy needs, as well as a discussion of wind energy economics, wind power and the environment, and organizations to contact for assistance. (2) *Small Wind Energy Systems Applications Guide*, 1993. Using case studies from around the world this guidebook discusses potential applications for small-scale wind energy technologies. (3) *1994-1995 Publications Catalog*. Lists the titles and descriptions of publications available from AWEA.

**U.S. Export Council on Renewable Energy (US/ECRE), 122 C St. NW, 4th floor, Washington, DC, 20001. Phone: 202-383-2550, Fax: 202-383-2555.**

*Renewable Energy Publications*. An annual catalog of technical reports, pamphlets, end-use brochures and product catalogues produced by US/ECRE member associations covering all types of renewable energy technologies.

**National BioEnergy Industries Association (NBIA), 122 C St. NW, 4th floor, Washington, DC 20001 USA. Phone: 202-383-2540, Fax: 202-383-2670.**

(1) *Biologue*. Published quarterly, this trade journal provides up-to-date coverage of policy and technology developments in the biomass energy field. (2) *Renewable Energy Publications Catalog*. A catalog of NBIA publications available by calling 202-383-2600.

**Solar Energy Industries Association (SEIA), 122 C St. NW, 4th floor, Washington, DC 20001, USA. Phone: 202-383-2600, Fax: 202-383-2670.**

(1) *Solar Industry Journal* The quarterly publication of the SEIA containing industry news, updates on research and developments, features on energy projects from the developing world, and energy facts and figures. (2) *Renewable Energy Fact Sheets*. A collection of reports on state-of-the-art developments in passive solar, photovoltaics, biomass fuels, and other renewable energies. (3) *1995 Catalogue of Renewable Energy Publications*. Contains titles and descriptions of publications available from SEIA including specialized reports on energy-efficient building in the Caribbean Basin and Latin America, Pacific Rim, and North Africa.

# The Contributors

### David L. Andersen

David L. Andersen is internationally known for his research and design work on ecotourism facilities and sustainable design strategies. He has presented papers and conducted workshops on ecotourism design around the world. He is a contributing author to numerous publications and has served as an ecotourism consultant to the Organization of American States in Guyana. He is past president of the Minneapolis Chapter American Institute of Architects, and he currently serves as a professional advisor to The Ecotourism Society.

### The ARA Consulting Group, Inc.
### (David Russell, Chris Bottrill, Greg Meredith)

The ARA Consulting Group, Inc., of Vancouver, Canada, has provided tourism consulting services worldwide for the last two decades. Recently the firm has emphasized marketing and product development for nature, culture and adventure tourism. The firm provides advice to the private sector and has assisted several Caribbean governments to establish self-financing national parks with strong linkages to ecotourism markets. As part of this effort, ARA has designed and constructed several interpretive facilities. On the marketing side, ARA has recently collaborated on the completion of a major market research effort in several North American cities to quantify ecotourism market potential for British Columbia and Alberta. ARA's services also include a management/environmental planning capability.

### Patricia Ashton

Patricia S. Ashton is associate director of Sustainable Tourism and Natural Resource Development Services for Water and Air Research, Inc. After teaching for five years and working at the Florida and North Carolina State Museums of Natural History as an associate curator in education, she began her career as the Director of International Field Expeditions for International Expeditions, Inc. Her work in Belize, Peru, Ecuador, China and Kenya brought her keen insight into community needs particularity in education. She is co-author of a number of publication on sustainable tourism development, including the Paseo Pantera Ecotourism Project's *An Introduction to Sustainable Tourism (Ecotourism) in Central America.*

### Ray Ashton

Ray Ashton is a scientist, educator and travel expert and is currently the director of Water and Air Research's Sustainable Tourism and Natural Resources Development Services. Over the past five years, he has traveled to 16 countries to provide consultant services in sustainable tourism and national park development. Most recently, he completed a milestone project in Honduras where he worked with the Honduran president and minister of tourism to create the first national park which will be totally financed by tourism and managed by a consortium of local people and government officials. He has published more than 100 scientific, educational, and popular books and articles and served as editor to a number of others.

### J. Thomas Atkins

A principal with Jones & Jones Architects and Landscape Architects of Seattle, Washington, Thomas Atkins has 25 years of national and international experience in large-scale open space planning and landscape architectural design projects in urban, rural and sensitive natural environments. He is presently working on several natural resource-based ecotourism development projects for the National Park System, the Tourism Bureau of Taiwan, the Washington Department of Transportation and private developers and land trusts.

### Alan Bair

Alan F. Bair, president of Pacific Yurts, Inc., studied art, architecture and literature at University of California and University of Paris-Sorbonne. In 1978, he founded Pacific Yurts, Inc., the original designer and manufacturer of the modern lattice-wall yurt, now used in recreation worldwide. Bair is 1994 Small Business Administration Exporter of the Year (Region X).

### Alan Bernstein

Alan Bernstein is deputy chairman and a cofounder of the Conservation Corporation, a conservation development company which owns and operates wildlife lodges in South Africa, Kenya, Tanzania and Zimbabwe.

A civil engineer by profession, Alan moved into the world of finance and investment banking in the U.K. and France before joining forces with well-known South African conservationist and ecotour operator, Dave Varty, to form the Conservation Corporation in 1990.

### Sam Bittman

Sam Bittman is president of BMG, Inc., a company that designs marketing strategies and integrated communications for responsible business, including organizations within the ecotourism industry. BMG is also active in the fields of health care, higher education and the arts. Bittman is the author of several gardening books including *The Salad Lover's Garden* (Doubleday, 1995) and has appeared on national television in connection with his work.

### Ralf Buckley

Ralf Buckley is director of the International Centre for Ecotourism Research and professor in the Faculty of Engineering and Applied Science at Griffith University in Queensland, Australia. He is also an adjunct professor in business, and director of the Centre for Environmental Management. He has worked in over 40 countries worldwide, and has over 15 years of experience in commercial consulting and private industry.

He has written extensively in professional journals, and has authored six books, including three on environmental planning, audit and management.

### Gerardo Budowski

Gerardo Budowski, The Ecotourism Society's second president, has long been in a leadership role in the world conservation community, where he has offered keen insights on the role tourism plays in the protection of natural resources. He is an authority in the field of conservation of the humid tropics, where he has first-hand experience with the full range of sustainable development alternatives.

### Susan D. Buse

Susan D. Buse currently serves as information specialist for The Ecotourism Society. She has assisted TES in coordinating and conducting ecotourism management workshops, has developed workshop curriculum resources, co-authored TES's *Annotated Bibliography for Planners and Managers* and organized TES's special collection of ecotourism resources at the George Washington University in Washington, DC. Buse has also conducted ecotourism research for the U.S.

National Park Service. She holds a Master of Science in Sustainable Development and Conservation Biology from the University of Maryland at College Park.

## Costas Christ

Costas Christ is the regional coordinator of The Ecotourism Society and the regional director for Africa Programs at the School for International Training. He is also the co-owner of Tamu Safaris, a nature tour operator. He has worked for the Kenya Wildlife Service and World Wildlife Fund and has written numerous articles on travel, ecotourism and international affairs for magazines and newspapers, including the *New York Times, International Herald Tribune* and *Sunday Times of London*. He has traveled extensively in Africa and Asia, where he was based for 14 years before returning to live in the United States.

## Michael M.S. Chun

Michael M.S. Chun, AIA, a principal of Wimberly Allison Tong & Goo, has directed national and international resort projects that have included the renowned Four Seasons Hotel, Newport Beach, California; the award-winning Grand Floridian Beach Resort at Disney World in Florida; and the Waterfront Hilton in Huntington Beach, California. Mr. Chun is currently principal for the Puerto del Sol Resort, Baja, California, Mexico; the Hans Lollik Island Resort, master plan and hotel, U.S. Virgin Islands; the Marriott at Cabo Negro, Isla de Margerita, Venezuela; the Baru Island Resort, master plan, Columbia; and the Amazon Rainforest Lodge, Brazil.

## Patricia Crow

Patricia Crow is a landscape architect working in New York City and is a graduate of Rhode Island School of Design and Harvard University Graduate School of Design where she was informed by the teachings of Carl Steinitz and Michael Binford on issues of sustainability. She was a contributor to the National Park Service's *Guideline for Sustainable Development* which was recently given an award by the American Society of Landscape Architects. While at Balmori Associates in New Haven, CT, she worked with the city of Farmington, Minnesota and the Design Center for American Urban Landscape to develop the Prairie Waterway, a created wetland and park for the city of Farmington. She is currently planning a study of the impacts on the landscape of a new ecotourism facility.

## Megan Epler Wood

Megan Epler Wood is the executive director of The Ecotourism Society (TES). She is one of the founders of TES and has been executive director since the organization was launched in 1990. Epler Wood has given presentations and conducted training workshops on ecotourism worldwide. She is the author of several publications on ecotourism, was the coordinator and editor of *Ecotourism Guidelines for Nature Tour Operators* and produced the PBS/Audubon special "The Environmental Tourist." Epler Wood is overseeing the development of Green Evaluations, a model monitoring program for nature tour operators, and heads the Ecolodge Forum and Field Seminar.

## Susan Everett

Susan Everett is director of the American Society of Landscape Architect's Department of Environmental Affairs. Everett was responsible for development of the ASLA Declaration on Environment and Development and is currently working with ASLA's Task Forces on Sustainable Development and International Affairs. Everett has undertaken collaborative land conservation and sustainable development initiatives with the Nature Conservancy, Pronatura (Mexico), Conservation International, the Trust for Public Land and the China Environmental Fund.

## Bob Galbreath

Bob Galbreath is a systems designer and president of Garden Technology, Inc. (GTI), a joint venturer in Geo-Lite Systems. He is responsible for the overall design of the Geo-Lite Ecolodge. His primary background is in the design of remote control systems for commercial applications. Galbreath is a member of the American Society of Agricultural Engineers.

## Cynthia Grippaldi

Cynthia Grippaldi has a background in environmental science and interpretation and energy efficient design and construction. She is a resident of St. John and a former employee of Maho Bay Camps. For the past three years, she has held the position of manager and supervisor of the Virgin Islands Environmental

Resource Station, an education and research field station on St. John operated by the University of the Virgin Islands.

### James Hadley

James Hadley is an architect practicing in New York City. He has worked in ecotourism since 1974 when he designed the initial layout and structures for Maho Bay Campgrounds on St. John in the U.S. Virgin Islands, working with Stanley Selengut. He has continued the relationship with Selengut, producing designs for Harmony and Estate Concordia – also on St. John – as well as projects for Grenada and the Florida Keys. His most recent work includes medical and transportation facilities and housing for homeless families.

### Donald E. Hawkins

As Professor of Tourism Studies at the George Washington University, Dr. Hawkins has contributed to the development of sustainable tourism planning and management education and research, with emphasis on ecotourism and cultural heritage tourism. He is the director of the International Institute of Tourism Studies, which was initiated in 1988, and is jointly sponsored by the World Tourism Organization. He was appointed the Dwight D. Eisenhower Professor of Tourism Studies in 1994. For The Ecotourism Society, he co-edited *Ecotourism: A Guide for Planners and Managers* with Kreg Lindberg in 1993 and served as conference director for the International Ecolodge Development Forum in 1994.

### Jasper (Joe) O. Hardesty

Joe Hardesty is a registered architect in Albuquerque, New Mexico and chairman of the Albuquerque Chapter American Institute of Architects Committee on the Environment. His company, Ecotecture: The Nature of the Built Environment, is a professional practice incorporating ecology plus architecture and planning, with an emphasis on sustainable design and development. Hardesty contributed to the design of the Estate Concordia Ecotents on St. John, U.S. Virgin Islands, and is currently designing an ecotourism resort for Puerto Rico.

### Kirk J. Iwanowski

Kirk J. Iwanowski is the cofounder and executive vice president of HVS Eco Services and the ECOTEL Certification Program, a division of Hotel Appraisals, Inc. (HVS). HVS Eco Services is an environmental and energy consulting and rating firm dedicated exclusively to the lodging industry. HVS Eco Services assists hotel owners and operators manage the rising costs associated with energy efficiency, water conservation, solid waste management and recycling, legislative compliance and employee environmental education and training. Iwanowski has lectured worldwide on the subject of environmentalism in the lodging industry. He is a graduate of the Cornell University School of Hotel Administration and has worked in many of the top hotels worldwide.

### Lani Kane

Lani Kane is a third-generation hotelier with extensive experience in the lodging and related leisure time industries. Ms. Kane joined Arthur Andersen after spending several years with the consulting divisions of Laventhol & Horwath and Landauer Associates in Miami. Her experience throughout the United States, the Caribbean and Mexico includes services from market evaluations, concept refinement/development and financial feasibility studies to tourism master plans, marketing programs and consumer research studies.

### Oswaldo Muñoz

Oswaldo Muñoz has been a naturalist guide for over 27 years and holds a degree in agronomy. He has recently started an agroecology project in the Ecuadorean highlands with local communities. Muñoz is also an instructor in guiding techniques and field interpretation, a free-lance writer on ecotourism and environmentalism, consultant to various conservation organizations, board member of The Ecotourism Society, president of Nuevo Mundo Expeditions and president of the Ecuadorean Ecotourism Association.

### John Reynolds

John Reynolds is deputy director for the National Park Service. He has also served as the Mid-Atlantic regional director of the Park Service, manager of the Denver Service Center (planning, design, construction), park superintendent at North Cascades National Park and assistant superintendent at Santa Monica Mountains National Recreation Area. Reynolds is a landscape architect and a fellow of the American Society of Landscape Architects.

### Elizabeth H. Richards

Elizabeth Richards is a mechanical engineer involved in various energy technologies at Sandia since 1980. Her past emphasis on photovoltaics research and development has led to involvement in the transfer of renewable energy technologies, both in the U.S. and in developing countries. She is co-author of "Solar Photovoltaics for Development Applications," and maintains a relationship with the U.S. Virgin Islands Energy Office. Richards has provided technical assistance in the long-term development of renewable energy systems for Harmony eco-resort and is currently manager of the Design Assistance Center's programs in Mexico.

### Chris Saumaiwai

Chris Saumaiwai, ethnomusicologist and managing director of Toys (Fiji) Ltd. specializing in teaching aids for preschools and aids for people with disabilities, has lived in the Fiji Islands documenting traditional Fijian music since 1965. Her husband is Fijian. Her project, Coral Coast Inn, is planned to provide a broad ecotourism experience designed to meet the needs of people with special needs.

### Stanley Selengut

Stanley Selengut is a civil engineer specializing in resort development. His varied career began in the 1950s when he created a large-volume importing company specializing in South American native crafts. Selengut's solutions to the developmental problems of South American villages led him to serve as a consultant to the Kennedy Administration. He completed 14 contracts in Latin America working for the State Department and then worked as staff consultant in Industrial Development for the Office of Economic Opportunity. On St. John, in the U.S. Virgin Islands, he created the 114-unit Maho Bay Campgrounds and Harmony, a center for the study of sustainable resort development.

### Craig R. Sholley

Craig R. Sholley's experiences with wildlife and travel began in 1973 as a Peace Corps Volunteer in Zaire, Africa. He has worked and traveled extensively since that time providing biological and ecotourism expertise in a variety of world arenas. He studied mountain gorillas with Dian Fossey at the celebrated Kariscke Research Center, after which he served as Curator of Education for the Baltimore Zoological Society. Sholley has led tours throughout Africa, South America and Asia. From late 1987, to 1990 he directed Rwanda's internationally known Mountain Gorilla Project, then acted as consulting zoologist for the award winning Imax film *Mountain Gorilla*. He has recently joined International Expeditions as director of Conservation and Education.

### Douglas White

20 years ago, after his first visit to the Virgin Islands, Doug White, AIA, decided to move to the Caribbean. He closed his New York City design studio and came to the Virgin Islands. On Tortola, he bought a classic 54' Sparkman & Stevens ocean racing yawl named *Stormy Weather*, moved aboard and went sailing for six years.

He has been practicing architecture for the past 14 years from his home/office overlooking Red Hook, in St. Thomas, specializing in the design of energy efficient vernacular buildings. He and his wife also own Caribbean Care, an environmentally friendly products and services company on St. Thomas.

### Peter Williams

Peter Williams is past chairman of the board and president of the Travel and Tourism Research Association. In the past five years, as director of the Centre for Tourism Policy and Research at Simon Fraser University, he has focused on issues including the relationship of the environment to tourism values and behavior, land-use planning and growth management. He received his Ph.D. from Utah State University.

### Robert Yearout

Robert Yearout is chief of the National Park Service Concession Program Division with oversight of the Service's concession and other commercial visitor services programs. Before coming to Washington, he most recently served as chief of the Service's Concession Planning and Analysis Division at the Denver Service Center, was a concession specialist at Grand Teton National Park and was a unit manager at Grand Canyon National Park.

# Index of Places